PASTORAL
Prayers
to Share

Year B

Also by David Sparks

Pastoral Prayers to Share, Year A

Prayers to Share, Year A

Prayers to Share, Year B

Prayers to Share, Year C

David Sparks

PASTORAL
PRAYERS
TO SHARE

Prayers of the People
for Each Sunday
of the Church Year

YEAR B

Revised Common
Lectionary Based

Editor: Ellen Turnbull
Cover and interior design: Verena Velten & Chaunda Daigneault
Cover photo: iStockphoto © Andrea Laurita
Proofreader: Dianne Greenslade

WoodLake is an imprint of Wood Lake Publishing, Inc. Wood Lake Publishing acknowledges the financial support of the Government of Canada, through the Book Publishing Industry Development Program (BPIDP) for its publishing activities. Wood Lake Publishing also acknowledges the financial support of the Province of British Columbia through the Book Publishing Tax Credit.

At Wood Lake Publishing, we practise what we publish, being guided by a concern for fairness, justice, and equal opportunity in all of our relationships with employees and customers. Wood Lake Publishing is committed to caring for the environment and all creation. Wood Lake Publishing recycles, reuses, and encourages readers to do the same. Resources are printed on 100% post-consumer recycled paper and more environmentally friendly groundwood papers (newsprint), whenever possible. A percentage of all profit is donated to charitable organizations.

Library and Archives Canada Cataloguing in Publication
Sparks, David, 1938-
Pastoral prayers to share, year B : prayers of the people for each Sunday of the church year / David Sparks.

"Revised common lectionary based".
Accompanied by a data CD.
Includes index.
Issued also in electronic format.
ISBN 978-1-55145-592-1

1. Pastoral prayers. 2. Church year--Prayer-books and devotions--English. I. Title.

BV250.S62 2011   264'.13   C2011-904248-7

Published by WoodLake
An imprint of Wood Lake Publishing Inc.
9590 Jim Bailey Road, Kelowna, BC, Canada, V4V 1R2
www.woodlakebooks.com
250.766.2778

Printing 10 9 8 7 6 5 4 3 2 1
Printed in Canada by
Houghton Boston

CONTENTS

GRATITUDES

My thanks go to those many persons at Wood Lake Publishing who have been involved in this *Pastoral Prayers* project.

I would especially like to mention Mike Schwartzentruber for gently encouraging me to start this venture, and Ellen Turnbull, editor, for her tireless, thoughtful, and empathetic presence in enabling the book to come to publication. She has made "the rough places smooth," and through her editorial efforts and initiatives this has become a far more faithful and useful book at the end than it was when we first began the creative journey.

Thanks also to Verena Velten for the dramatically inspiring cover design and Chaunda Daigneault for her skilled work on the layout of the book. It is good to look at and easy to use.

Thanks to my wife, Kathy, for her loving support and encouragement in the long days of this writing project.

It is the people of the congregations where I have led worship that have shaped and inspired these prayers. Their joys, their sorrows, their dreams and testing times, their challenges, and their responses to the Christian year are mirrored in my words and prayer phrases. It is a huge responsibility to offer prayer Sunday by Sunday, and it has been the support of so many wonderful "persons of the pew," and their willingness to explore ways of offering pastoral prayer, that made this book possible. I am deeply grateful.

INTRODUCTION

I have been encouraged and heartened by the response of worship leaders to the three volumes of *Prayers to Share*. These books have found a home on many a worship leader's bookshelf in North America, but also as far afield as the United Kingdom, Australia, and India.

As I participated in prayer workshops after the release of the books, many people told me that they found the responsive format very useful; it allowed congregational members and worship leaders to have a common involvement in the prayer offering. I also heard one particular question asked time and time again: "So what about pastoral prayers? We need some help with them as well!"

This lectionary-based book is a response to that often-voiced request.

My conversations with worship leaders identified that most leaders find the retyping of words into a computer file very tedious! Thus, each print volume of *Pastoral Prayers to Share* includes a data CD for easy copying or manipulation of the material for printing or projection.

The online version of this volume of prayers has the same capability as the data CD. The transfer of prayer data can be done easily and swiftly and the task of modifying the prayer can be accomplished as and when the worship leader chooses.

Some worship leaders are not sure about the freedom to reproduce the prayers either in their existing or modified form. Put simply, you may reproduce any prayer included in this book for use within your own congregation without seeking the authority of anyone. If you intend to include a portion of the book in another publication, *you will need to contact Wood Lake Publishing for permission.*

As this book is the second of a series of three, the author and the publisher would welcome feedback on what might be changed or incorporated into the subsequent volume for lectionary year C. Please send your comments to:

Ellen Turnbull
Editor
Wood Lake Publishing Inc.
9590 Jim Bailey Road
Kelowna BC V4V 1R2
ellent@woodlake.com

The pastoral prayer is a common enterprise of faith. Worship leaders and people together have the responsibility of offering to God those situations, persons, and challenges that concern our hearts, our minds, and our essential spirit.

We faithfully offer our prayers Sunday by Sunday in a world where the inroads of our materialistic society threaten to erode completely the ancient and treasured life of faith. But does it do any good to pray for the world and its needs? Does it do any good to pray for our own needs? Could we not be doing something more useful? Will the next generation be a praying generation?

The questions will continually come to us, but at the end of the day we can only look to the one all-loving God and say, "We cannot cease from praying."

ABOUT PASTORAL PRAYER

What are we attempting to do when we pray for others?"

What we are *not* trying to do is persuade God to act in a particular way in the world, or fulfill the wishes of the members of the faith community who are praying, or get ourselves out of taking some initiative or doing some work. That is, we are not trying to persuade God to do what we ourselves could do with some energy and effort.

So what *are* we about as pastoral *pray*-ers?

We are about bringing ourselves individually and as a faith community into right relationship with God. We do this because it is a necessary first step to fulfilling God's intention for Earth's inhabitants: the establishment of God's realm or kingdom. Jesus makes this intention the central theme of his teaching.

We are about expressing our compassion for suffering humanity. This is a basic need and desire for those who follow Jesus Christ.

It is natural to express to God what is on our hearts, and to do so in company with faith community friends who share the same beliefs. In the same way that we rush to tell a best friend or well-loved family member of our joys and deepest concerns, so without a moment's thought do we bring them to God. Even persons with no formal religious belief pray fervently to God when the chips are down!

We are about being willing to be involved in the answers to our own prayers. In his book *The Use of Praying,* J. Neville Ward puts the concept very well. He writes that our prayers are "a piece of work involving costly self-surrender for God, for the work God wants done on other souls." And so we are challenged every time we offer or hear prayer to ask ourselves, "What can we do to enable the outcome that will bring God's realm closer?" So...*there is a famine in Ethiopia.* It is on the TV news night after night. It comes up in the pastoral prayer. We know that Ethiopia is thousands of miles away in Africa and we cannot personally take food and water to those who are suffering, but we are able to financially support the International Red Cross, or Doctors without Borders, who are able to care for the victims.

So…*a phrase in the pastoral prayer catches our attention.* It speaks of the need to "help those who are reluctant to go to the doctor" for consultation. The phrase reminds us of a friend who is agonizing over a persistent back pain; as a result of hearing the prayer (or writing it) we call up the friend and are with her in her decision to seek medical advice.

So…*a phrase in the prayer speaks of the need to support leaders in our local faith community.* We hear a call within the prayer to offer a word of thanks to those who serve our church without fuss, and to consider leadership within the church ourselves.

So…*a phrase in the prayer reminds us of the fact that God never leaves us in times when we feel depressed.* We have a close family member who is "in the dark valley." It is a stimulus to make that visit that we have been promising to make for a week or so. Or it may be that we are personally feeling low and need reassurance that God is with us in our miserable moments.

One responsibility as worship leader is to provide education about the significance and meaning of the pastoral prayer. It does not have the prominence in the service of the sermon, or the popularity of congregational song or hymns, and is often seen as one last thing to do before the final hymn and blessing. I have heard of one worship leader who will, if the service is running a little late, leave the pastoral prayer out altogether! I am certain that there is a need to regularly explain the purpose of the pastoral prayer to members of the congregation, and that they will be grateful for the explanation and feel more involved as the prayer is offered.

HOW TO USE THIS BOOK
A step-by-step guide

The Prayers in This Book

Most of the time, each prayer is divided into four sections: prayers for the world, prayers for the suffering, prayers for the church/faith, and prayers for ourselves. This split into four divisions gives a consistent structure to the pastoral prayer and enables the worship leader to make changes and substitutions easily. Icons in the margin allow for quick identification of the sections:

World	Suffering	Church	Ourselves
Prayers for the world, including prayers for persons or groups of persons in the local town, city, or municipality, and the neighbourhood.	*Prayers for the suffering*, including prayers for those who have suffered loss, those who are sick, those who are caregivers, the bereaved, and those who support them.	*Prayers for the church/faith community*, the local church, wider church groupings, and faith communities supported by mission money throughout the world.	*Prayers for ourselves.* Acknowledging the fact that persons worshipping have specific needs and want these to be recognized in the worship.

Preparing to Offer Public Pastoral Prayer

Many diligent worship leaders will take time to review the scripture passages weeks or months ahead of the appropriate Sunday. Often this review will coincide with a fresh season in the church year. The purpose is often to consider sermon themes, but it also provides an opportunity to consider pastoral prayers and reflect on how they might be offered.

When you are offering a pastoral prayer on any given Sunday it is good to begin to think about the prayer no later than Monday morning of that week. A part of the preparation could be to read aloud the appropriate lectionary scriptures for that week and silently reflect on them.

During the week, as you encounter friends, and church and family members and reflect with them on their joys, sorrows, frustrations, and challenges, remember that there may be a place for their situations in your pastoral prayer. And as you reflect on your own feelings and circumstances (the crisis at work, the bullying of one of your children at school), remember that these too could find a place in the prayer you offer.

As you read the newspaper, as you check the news on your computer, smartphone, or television, be alert for items that make an impact on you or others. It could be an earthquake, or conflict in the Middle East, or a local item such as an interview with the parents of a missing young person. If the story has people talking or arguing, or has an emotional impact, then it could form a phrase of the pastoral prayer.

There are aspects of offering public prayer that you need to carefully guard. **The privacy laws in your area or country should be strictly followed.** It is usually not permissible to mention the names of those who are in local hospitals or care homes unless you have their express permission. And the same goes for family members, especially children; be sure that you ask them directly if you want to include them or their situation in your prayer. Do not assume that they will not find out if they are not in church at the time of the pastoral prayer. They will!

If you are the sort of person who is well-organized, keep a notebook beside your desk or in your pocket. It is helpful to jot down pastoral prayer ideas and topics as they come to you.

Give the pastoral prayer a regular place in your personal prayer life. Pray by name for those who are on your mind or in your heart, and who you need to hold up before God. Also listen out for those promptings that come to you in significant times of holy silence.

In this book, the language used is inclusive of gender as it relates to persons and as it relates to God. I would encourage you, the worship leader, to avoid a preference for male imagery and male pronouns.

I would also encourage you to carefully monitor the words that you use in prayer. For me, the comment in the preface to *The Good News Bible* is a good guide: "Every effort has been made to use language that is natural, clear, simple, and unambiguous." Most persons in the pew these days don't understand, or misinterpret, words such as *righteousness* and *redemption*. A good rule of thumb is to use words that appear in your daily newspaper or are used during the television news.

At the end of the day, remember the words of Thomas Merton: We do not want to be beginners [at prayer]. But let us be convinced of the fact that we will never be anything but beginners, all our life!

Different Formats

There are many ways to offer pastoral prayer. In most of the formats in this book the scripture readings (usually the gospel reading) for lectionary year B provide the theme for the prayer.

The format used most often in this book is the two leaders/ congregational response format. *The words of the first leader are printed in bold italic*. The words of the second leader are printed in regular type. **The words of the congregational response are printed in bold.**

Format 1: Two leaders with congregational response

One: We live in Advent hope, O God.
We await the coming of Jesus to our world.
Two: Jesus is here when there is permanent peace.
Jesus is here when the poor amongst us are supported, and the developmentally and physically challenged are free to enjoy a fulfilled life.
Jesus is here when those with resources give gifts to those stressed for lack of holiday money.
Jesus is here when the wisdom of children is listened to and heeded.
In an uneasy world,

> *One:* *we will work faithfully*
> **All:** **to free the spirit of Jesus, God's Anointed One.**

NOTES

The trigger phrase *we will work faithfully* and congregational response **to free the spirit of Jesus, God's Anointed One** would be printed in the bulletin or projected.

The prayer may be also be offered by a single worship leader – simply ignore the bold italics.

Format 2: One leader with congregational response
and
Format 3: A personal (feeling) reflection on the Christian scriptures

(How we wish we could have been on Jordan's bank!)

One: How we wish we could have been on Jordan's bank!
On Jordan's bank was a crowd of people seeking radical change in their life's direction.
We pray for those who face medical conditions that are difficult to diagnose or treat.
We pray for those who are held back by guilt over past wrongs, and for those who need the help of another to reveal their hidden gifts and talents.
We pray for those in spiritual crisis, who seek renewal and inspiration in their shadowed times.
We pray for those who find life fragmented and overwhelming.
We pray for those who are sick, for whom each new day is a struggle.
We pray for those who have lost loved ones and find it hard to break out of the tomb of bereavement (*time of silent reflection*).
As we pray that forgiveness and empowerment will be the reality for ourselves and for our friends,
Two: *how we wish,*
All: **we could have been on Jordan's bank!**

Format 4: Use the key words of scripture as a peg on which to hang the prayer.

Isaiah 35, selected verses indicated by *

One: *This is our hope, O God, that, "the ransomed of the Lord will return, and come to Zion with singing."* *

Two: This is our hope, O God, that revival will burst out in our faith communities, and vibrant worship and selfless service will be marks of our local and mission projects. This is our hope, O God, that faith communities will serve together in the local community.

One: *It seems a far-off hope,*

All: **but with faithful effort, it will become joyful reality.**

One: *This is our hope, O God, that, "they shall obtain joy and gladness, and sorrow and sighing will flee away."* *

Two: This is our hope, O God, that the fears which hold us bound will be faced, and the talents we keep hidden will be used. This is our hope, O God, that the anxiety that we do not speak of will be expressed, and worries about family members will be shared.

One: *It seems a far-off hope,*

All: **but with faithful effort, it will become joyful reality.**

Format 5: Use people and objects to illustrate and emphasize.

White Gift Service Intergenerational Prayer
An Eyes-Open Prayer to be prayed slowly.

A young person holds up battered rag doll, while another holds up a new computer game in a shiny box.

One: We pray for boys and girls who have few gifts this Christmas.

All: **Help us, O God, to help them.**

The young person with the shiny toy gives it to the one with the rag doll.

An adult holds up a packet of pasta, while another holds up a fancy box of chocolates.
> One: We pray for families for whom Christmas will just be
>   another tough day.
> **All: Help us, O God, to share with them.**

The person with the chocolates exchanges them for the pasta.

Format 6: Follow the theme of the scripture.

Isaiah 7:10–16
Matthew 1:18–25

Jesus is born to Mary. Joseph has a dream.

> One: **Jesus is born to Mary. Joseph dreams of a saviour.**
>   **The world will never be the same again!**
> Two: Families living below the poverty line receive
>   government help, and challenged children get the
>   support they need.
>   Women and men labouring in sweatshops earn a fair
>   wage in a safe and clean workplace.
>   Those who speak another language are treated with
>   respect, and those from different cultural backgrounds
>   are given the opportunity to follow their trade or
>   profession.
>   A lack of money is no longer a barrier to higher
>   education, nor influence the way to a secure job.
> One: *Jesus was born the Saviour,* ·
> **All: and we will bring salvation in our own time.**

Format 7: Base the prayer on a hymn.

For example, sing a verse of *In Suffering Love (Voices United* #614) before each section.

> **All: Sing verse one:** *In suffering love the thread of life...*
> One: *In suffering love,*
> Two: we pray for those who are caught up in the conflicts of
>   our world in (*insert current event*).
> One: *In suffering love,*

Two: we pray for those for whom the basic necessities of life
cannot be taken for granted.
We think of those forced to live on the streets because
there is no suitable housing.

All: Sing verse two: *There is a rock, a place secure…*
One: *In suffering love,*
Two: we pray for those within the church who are going
through hard times; those in the wider church for
whom the support of the mission fund is the difference
between a fulfilling life or a meagre existence.

Format 8: Use part of a hymn as the congregational response.

Prayer of Thanksgiving
The people's chorus is the first verse of *Now Thank We All Our God*
(Voices United #236).

One: *Thanks beyond measure, O Most Gracious God,*
for those who join us around the table today and
tomorrow, and for those family members and friends
who cannot be with us
Two: because of the cost of travel,
because of ill health,
because of conflict,
because they live so far away.
Thank you, God, for family and friends.
All sing: Now thank we all our God, with heart, and
hands and voices…

Format 9: Make the prayer fully responsive.

One: God is alive!
We see God stressed with the military forces and
civilians in a warzone *(current area of conflict).*
All: How much danger do they have to endure?
One: We see God despairing about the refugees in Darfur
Sudan.
All: Will nobody give them the attention they deserve?
One: We see God juggling home and work with the parents of
young children.

All: Are there enough hours in the day?
      God is alive! We are on God's side.

 One: God is alive!
      We find God sitting frustrated in an overcrowded
      emergency department. .
All: **We find God struggling with an unforeseen diagnosis.**
One: We find God on the ward with overworked medical
      staff.
All: **We find God with a bereaved person coming to**
      terms with a harsh new reality.
One: We think of those we know who are suffering (*time of*
      silent reflection).
All: **God is alive! We are on God's side.**

NOTE:

The fully responsive format will be the natural way to go when a
projected version of the liturgy is used,

Format 10: Use silence for effect.

The Parable of the Sower – A Pastoral Prayer

One: Stony ground: the continuing distrust between faith
      groups in our nation and in the world; the hate bred by
      prejudice and ignorance.
All: **Stony ground: those affected by acts of terrorism**
      in (*current situation*) (*time of silent reflection*).
One: Stony ground: illness that will not yield to treatment,
      delay in treating needy patients due to staff shortages.
      We think of those we know who are ill (*time of silent*
      reflection). These persons are on our minds.
All: **Stony ground: frustrating relationships, family**
      differences for which there seem no resolution, no
      change.
One: Stony ground: the barren, empty place of bereavement.
      We think of those we know who have lost loved ones
      (*time of silent reflection*). These persons are in our
      hearts.

All: Stony ground: that feeling of being stuck in
       circumstances that cannot be changed.
One: Stony ground: fears hidden deep within us that cannot
      be released.
All: Stony ground: a faith life that is stale and
       unrewarding (*time of reflection*).
One: If we can identify the stony ground, we have taken the
      first step in bringing change.
All: Loving God, may renewed determination bring a
       harvest of new opportunity and new direction.
       May a willingness to express our fears bring
       a harvest of freedom. May an exploration
       into aspects of our faith bring a joyful and
       spiritual harvest.

Format 11: The prayer is read silently by the congregation.

The leader begins the prayer with a simple phrase, such as, "Death is defeated, Jesus lives." In *silence* the congregation reads the subsequent phrases printed in the bulletin or projected. Then the leader says the trigger phrase, and the congregation responds.

One: ***The tomb is empty. Jesus lives!*** *(Or after Easter*
      *Sunday use, **Death is defeated, Jesus lives.**)*
      Leave 45–60 seconds silence for reading and reflection.
All: *read the following in silence*

read in silence {
      The world will be a better place!
      The peacemakers will find a way to end the fighting in
      (*current example*).
      The reasons for the abuse and neglect of seniors living
      alone will be determined, and action taken.
      Hope will come to the homeless in our area through (*local*
      initiatives).
      Struggling students will find a person who enlivens their
      studies.

One: ***Jesus lives,***
All: **hope is alive!**

Format 12: Use physical action as part of the prayer.

Good Friday

All: **We come to the cross** (a nail is hammered into a wooden cross),
we look up (a nail is hammered in),
we see the broken Christ (a nail is hammered in),

One: and we pray for those broken in our world.
We pray for refugees who have had to flee from their homes and communities.
We pray for boys forced to fight, and girls forced into prostitution.
We pray for those hated by their neighbours or bullied by their peers.
We pray for the broken,

All: **and God calls us to reflection and to action.**

Format 13: Dialogue with the congregation before one or more of the prayer sections.

Proper 13 Year B John 6:24–35: This is the gospel passage where Jesus tells people that he is the bread of life.

Engage the congregation in dialogue about hunger and then use the prayer from Proper 14 as a guide to crafting a prayer. Make the point that hunger is a basic human condition and ask about times when individuals in the congregation have been hungry. Then broaden the discussion to include those in our world who are hungry right now.

Talk of the word "hunger" as it refers to "deep longing" – a hunger for shelter for the transients in our community, or a hunger for improved daycare facilities. In the Suffering section, consider the hunger for improved emergency treatment that might exist in your community, or a deep hunger for a hospice where the dying are treated with dignity. The Church section might reveal a hunger for people to sing the old hymns more often, or for an outreach study group to be held in a local library or store.

It will be useful to have two persons involved in this dialogue (as well as the congregation); one to talk with the congregation and another to shape a prayer.

The prayer might look something like this:

We recognize that hunger is part of each of us, Loving God. We recognize that in our world there are many hungers. We heard from Louise about hunger in Ethiopia and the efforts of the United Nations to provide food and the means of production. We pray for the people of Ethiopia and the United Nations efforts, and help them by donating money.

Jeff has reminded us of hunger nearer home and of the St. Andrew's United Church food bank. We pray for the volunteers who run the food bank, and for the families who now have food.

Ginny has spoken of the shortage of daycare spaces. *Little Tykes* is full now and has a waiting list. We pray for those advocating for an expansion to *Little Tykes*, and we welcome their petition.

Loving God, you satisfy our deepest hungers.

Format 14: Dramatization

Dramatization brings the prayer alive and ensures it is remembered. This may mean that the prayer lasts longer. Why not have a shorter sermon that week? For example:

Proper 24 year B: The requests of James and John to have the top places when Jesus comes in glory.

Dr. Dave Jones: Well, my job is more important than yours. People come to me with life-threatening illnesses. It wouldn't be much good if they brought a bleeding person to your church office!

Rev. Jim Smith: True, but when that same person is dying, your prescription won't be worth the paper it's written on. She'll need someone who speaks of life that goes on when earthly life is over. She'll need a priest or minister. Who will be the important one then?

Nancy Pravic: Cut it out you two! Stop trying to out-do one another! You both have God-given gifts. You use them at different, equally important times. The key question is whether you are willing to serve needy persons carefully and compassionately when the occasion arises.

Format 15: The extemporary prayer

The previous ways of offering pastoral prayer assume that the worship leader will follow a format set down in printed form. It may be used as a template and adjusted, but the basic form will be followed.

The extemporary prayer is offered by the worship leader without any printed guide. Sometimes the prayer is the result of much prayerful preparation, and sometimes the worship leader relies on the Holy Spirit to directly guide him/her in what he/she is to say at the pastoral prayer time of the service.

Faithfully offered extemporary pastoral prayers are wonderful. Those offered by a thoroughly prepared worship leader with confidence in his/her ability to pray freely are most effective, but the worship leader who has done little or no preparation and relies on "the Spirit" to get him/her out of trouble usually ends up with an ineffective and long-winded prayer.

The controversy over the use of a written form of prayer versus praying extemporaneously has been going on for centuries. The 17th-century diarist Samuel Pepys records that he was in a "hot dispute" with the ship's chaplain about extemporary prayer on a voyage to Holland back in 1660.

The worship leader who has no experience in offering extemporary prayer would do well to try out the medium in a safe environment before using it in a worship service. Prayer offered at the end of a time of small group learning in the faith community might be a way of getting started.

A good rule of thumb is to use extemporaneous prayer in public worship only when you feel confident and comfortable enough to do so.

Format 16: Devise your own prayer.

Feel free to experiment and improvise with your own ways of offering prayer.

As worship leader, the prayer is yours and you may add, alter, or delete the suggested text as you wish. Perhaps there are one or more of the phrases that you feel need changing in light of current or world or community situations. Feel free to make the changes. Perhaps the responsive phrase at the end of the prayer does not work for you. Replace it with a responsive phrase that rings true.

Perhaps one word sums up for you the essence of the whole gospel reading for that Sunday. Compose a prayer with that word in mind and trust the source of your inspiration and your own words.

As worship leader, you have your unique prayer voice, and the pastoral prayer is one of the places in the service to find and develop it. Don't be afraid to experiment with different forms of prayer, or to use words or illustrations that feel right but that you haven't used before.

A good rule of thumb is to ask yourself if the members of the congregation will remember the prayer when they get home. And more importantly, will the prayer inspire them to get involved in the answer to one or more of the prayer issues?

Go to it!

SEASON OF ADVENT
Advent 1

(Begins on the first Sunday of Advent in 2011, 2014, 2017, 2020...)

LECTIONARY READINGS
Isaiah 64:1–9
Psalm 80:1–7, 17–19
1 Corinthians 1:3–9
Mark 13:24–37

Be watchful, and stay faithful until the end.

You call us to be on the lookout, O God,
for the ominous signs:
When concern for the environment is considered less
  important than profit;
When returns to the shareholders are considered more
  important than care of the employees;
Where corruption in government is ignored or hidden;
Where the powerless and despised are ignored and
  downtrodden.
We are your guardians, O God,
and we stand ready to speak out and act.

You call us to be on the lookout, O God,
for the ominous signs:
The older person finding it harder to cope with everyday tasks;
The troubled one who will not seek skilled help;
The young one who is defiant and disrespectful;
The despised ones who lack food or a safe place to live;
The struggling sick and bereaved persons in our own family or
  in our church family *(we remember them silently or out loud).*
We are your guardians, O God,
and we stand ready to speak out and act.

You call us to be on the lookout, O God,
for the ominous signs:
Persons who speak of welcome but do not act in a welcoming
  way;

Persons who find it difficult to look beyond this faith
community and its building;
Persons whose worship is rooted in the way "it's always been
done";
Persons who are willing to give to local needs but will not
consider giving to mission work.
We are your guardians, O God,
And we stand ready to speak out and act.

You call us to be on the lookout, O God,
for the ominous signs in ourselves:
A reluctance to admit and learn from our mistakes;
An unwillingness to open our eyes to new realities at home or
in church;
A narrow vision when it comes to helping those in need;
A lack of enthusiasm when it comes to supporting or helping
those at risk in our community.
We will listen to your guardians, O God,
when they call on us to speak out and act.

Another Way

**1. The first Sunday in Advent is often celebrated as the Hope
Sunday.**

We live in Advent hope, O God, we live in hope.
We live in hope that those affected by floods/drought/famine
(use a current event) will find long-term partnership and
relief.
We live in hope that those without a job will get the retraining
and encouragement they need.
We live in hope that aboriginal persons in this country will get
the respect, education, and practical help they need.
We live in hope that political prisoners will be noticed and will
find active support.
We hear the cries of the oppressed and downhearted,
and we will help their heartfelt hopes become reality.

We live in Advent hope, O God, we live in hope.
We live in hope that those who are financially challenged at Christmas will seek help.
We live in hope that those who are troubled and depressed will find a listening presence and an understanding shoulder to cry on.
We live in hope that those who are sick or in hospital will know peace in the pain-filled hours and will sense your uplifting and sustaining presence.
We live in hope that members of our own family and members of our church family will find healing and peace. We remember in the silence of our hearts those who are sick or troubled *(time of silent reflection).*
We live in the *eternal* hope that those who have died are safe in your loving presence, and that the bereaved will be comforted.
We will be among those who see the opportunity for change for good, for
we hear the cries of the oppressed and downhearted,
and we will help their heartfelt hopes become reality.

 We live in Advent hope, O God, we live in hope.
We live in hope that the Christian way will become a life-building way for many in our town and the surrounding area.
We live in hope that our church will work with other churches to find those most at risk in our neighbourhood and help them.
We live in hope that the wider church, the national church, may never lose sight of the needs of the faith communities beyond our nation's shores, and through mission funds will support their needs.
We live in hope that the life-giving values of your Realm will take root in our society.
We will take our place among faith community members who are committed to building up the church, for
we hear the cries of the oppressed and downhearted,
and we will help their heartfelt hopes become reality.

We live in Advent hope, O God, each one of us lives in hope.
We live in hope that our hidden talents will be revealed and
  put to work in ways that are faithful.
We live in hope that in the testing times that come with illness
  and old age we will maintain a positive and lively spirit.
We live in hope that our family and loved ones will face up to
  their challenges, and be ready to share their doubts.
We live in hope that we will believe in ourselves despite
  having feelings that deny our self-worth and our sense of
  worth in your sight.
We live in hope that as life ends we will know your love
  around us, for us, and with us.
**We live in hope, for in Jesus Christ we see that your
  hope for the world, O God,
is human, practical, and positive. Thank you!**

2. Choose one verse of an Advent hymn or song to sing after
   each section of the prayer. Or sing all the verses, one after
   each section. Examples: *Hope Shines as the Solitary Star* (*More
   Voices* #220), or *I Am Walking a Path of Peace/Hope/Joy* (*More
   Voices* #221), or *Hope Is a Star* (*Voices United* #7).

Advent 2

LECTIONARY READINGS
Isaiah 40:1–11
Psalm 85:1–2, 8–13
2 Peter 3:8–15a
Mark 1:1–8

> *The good news about Jesus is revealed by
> the prophetic voice in the wilderness.*

Prepare for God's promised one!
The promised one has a message to change the world:
That the poorest and most disadvantaged are honoured by
    God; we think of those in…
That the vulnerable and mentally challenged are precious in
    God's sight. In particular, we remember…
That the most selfish and single-minded are not beyond
    forgiveness; this week we think of *(situation of forgiveness).*
The longest and most hate-provoking wars and racial conflicts
    can be settled, such as …
This is Good News!
We stand with John, and wait for the coming of Jesus.

Prepare for God's promised one!
The promised one has a message for the suffering:
That even the most tongue-tied and shy will be noticed;
That the elderly and the young are worthy of respect;
That God's love for the seriously ill is steadfast; we remember
    in silence now *(time of silent reflection);*
That God is with the dying and those who wait with them;
That God stands beside the bereaved, who we remember in
    silence now *(time of silent reflection).*
This is Good News!
We stand with John, and wait for the coming of Jesus.

Prepare for God's promised one!
The promised one has a message to inspire the church:
That God's word still is relevant and urgent;
That it takes just a few committed followers to make a world
    of difference;

That the downhearted need encouragement;
That those who are full of self-importance are not as
  important as they see themselves to be.
This is Good News!
We stand with John, and wait for the coming of Jesus.

Prepare for God's promised one!
The promised one has a message for each one of us:
That we stand in a long tradition of Christian saints;
That we have gifts to give and use in God's service;
That we know and can promote the values of God's realm –
  justice, peace, and sharing;
That nothing can separate us from the love of God.
This is Good News!
We stand with John, and wait for the coming of Jesus.

Another Way

1. **The second Sunday in Advent is often celebrated as the Peace
   Sunday.**

John's good news about Jesus is the best news for us.
In the struggle there is a promise of peace:
In the current discussions between *(could be labour
  negotiations, Middle East conflict, local issues)*;
Where environmentalists and polluters sit down together;
Where journalists reveal fresh evidence of corruption or
  bribery;
Where there is dissention over a community or
  neighbourhood issue *(detail a local issue)*.
***In the honest expression of views, in the will for justice and
  healing,***
we give thanks for the promise of peace.

John's good news about Jesus is the best news for us.
In the struggle there is a promise of peace:
In the conflicting views of those who are victims of crime and
  those who commit crime;
In the clamour for adequate medical services;

In the advocacy for adequate low cost housing;
In the support for low income families;
In the refusal to label anyone as "handicapped."
*In the honest expression of views, in the will for justice and
    healing,*
we give thanks for the promise of peace.

John's good news about Jesus is the best news for us.
In the struggle there is a promise of peace:
In facing the reality of illness;
In the hard place standing beside the sick and suffering;
In the responsibility of caring for elderly and infirm parents;
In the patient attempts of parents to guide, direct, and provide
    healthy choices for their children;
And in the lonely place of bereavement *(time of silent
    reflection).*
*In the honest expression of views, in the will for justice and
    healing,*
we give thanks for the promise of peace.

*John's good news about Jesus is the best news for each one
    of us.*
In the struggle there is a promise of peace.
When we feel that we have failed in our responsibilities as
    workers or parents or church members,
When we feel stuck in an unhelpful attitude or approach,
When we cannot shake the apathy or depression that
    controls us,
When we dwell on a mistake long gone but not forgotten,
For the advice of a wise counsellor,
For the support of a friend,
For the renewed will to leave the past in the past,
we give thanks for the promise of peace.

2. Sing the first verse of *On Jordan's Bank* (*Voices United* #20),
   or use *Wait for the Lord* (*Voices United* #22) after each section
   of the prayer. Or use the refrain of *All Who Are Thirsty* (*More
   Voices* #4) after each section.

Advent 3

LECTIONARY READINGS
Isaiah 61:1–4, 8–11
Psalm 126 **or** Luke 1:47–55
1 Thessalonians 5:16–24
John 1:6–8, 19–28

*John tells of the true light and prepares the way for
God's amazing gift in Jesus.*

Jesus the true light. *(The Christ candle is raised high.)*
In this revealing light, people and communities change:
Leaders who abuse the power of their authority and position
 find humility;
Those who hoard their wealth and resources find generosity;
Struggling single parents and those on welfare or minimum
 wage find support from food banks and community
 organizations;
Silent cries for friendship find a listening ear;
The questions of young persons are taken seriously.
You have seen the true light.
**We see the true light in Jesus; we will be a leading light
 to others.**

Jesus the true light. *(The Christ candle is raised high.)*
In this revealing light the suffering find relief:
Those uncertain of the way out of addiction find a group to
 accompany and support them;
Persons afraid to go to a doctor about a troubling problem find
 the courage to make an appointment;
Families in financial difficulties seek out credit counsellors;
The sick and mentally troubled receive the help they need;
And the bereaved find that friends are with them in the empty
 place *(time of silent reflection).*
You have seen the true light.
**We see the true light in Jesus; we will be a leading light
 to others.**

Jesus the true light. *(The Christ candle is raised high.)*
In this revealing light the community of faith searches for the
way ahead:
Churches try out fresh patterns of worship with an emphasis
on silence or singing;
Churches make contact with their neighboring faith
communities and eat and learn together;
Churches promote mission enterprises and support them as
generously as they do local ones;
Churches remember their neighbourhood setting and ask their
neighbours how the church can help them.
You have seen the true light.
**We see the true light in Jesus; we will be a leading light
to others.**

 Jesus the true light. *(The Christ candle is raised high.)*
In this revealing light each one of us is challenged to learn and
grow and change:
We welcome insights into our personality and ways of being
with others;
We welcome fresh opportunities to learn at work and serve in
our leisure time;
We welcome the chance to make amends for a past wrong and
receive the forgiveness of another.
We welcome word that reminds us of the central place of the
spiritual in our lives
and the need to give time and space to God in our day.
You have seen the true light.
**We see the true light in Jesus; we will be a leading light
to others.**

Another Way

1. **The third Sunday in Advent is often celebrated as
the Joy Sunday.**

**Use the first phrase of the well-known Advent hymn *Good
Christian Friends, Rejoice* (*Voices United* #35). Once you get
into the rejoice and thanksgiving grooves, your own ideas will
flow easily into the format below.**

All sing: *Good Christian friends, rejoice with heart and soul and voice!*

One: Rejoice that people are working hard to find a way to peace in...

Two: Rejoice that those who want to find a way to keep our planet green and cool are being listened to.

One: Rejoice that people are giving money to (*for example, the Salvation Army kettles in our city*). Rejoice that those with plenty are responding to appeals to help those with so little.

Two: *Talk about a current "good news" item.*

Young person: Rejoice! This is awesome!

Mother or Father: Rejoice! And thank God!

Grandparent or older person: Rejoice! And get busy!

All sing: *Good Christian friends, rejoice with heart and soul and voice!*

One: Rejoice that research into cancers and heart problems is making progress that was unthinkable a generation ago.

Rejoice that older persons with dementia and infirmities are getting the respect they are due.

Rejoice that people are coming to terms with their medical problems.

We remember those members of our families who are in hospital or sick at home *(time of silent reflection)*.

Two: Rejoice that (*the local medical or nursing school*) is training its students well.

Or, rejoice that medical professionals and personal care workers are getting the continuing training they need.

One: Rejoice that there are people ready to listen to those who have lost loved ones. We remember those in our congregation who have lost loved ones. We are glad with them for many good memories *(time of silent reflection)*.

Young person: Rejoice! This is awesome!

Mother or Father: Rejoice! And thank God!

Grandparent or older person: Rejoice! And get busy!

All sing: *Good Christian friends, rejoice with heart and soul and voice!*

One: Rejoice in the skills and commitment of the leadership in our church at this time.

Two: *Rejoice that our White Gifts will make lots of people happy.*

Rejoice in the carols, songs, and readings that warm our
hearts in Advent and Christmas worship services; rejoice in
the silence, rejoice in the candlelight.

One: Rejoice that all over the world our mission gifts will
bring hope to people who struggle and are afraid, and who
need to know the spirit of Jesus Christ is with them.

Two: *Speak of a specific mission project supported by wider
church funds.*

Young person: Rejoice! This is awesome!

Mother or Father: Rejoice! And thank God!

Grandparent or older person: Rejoice! And get busy!

*All sing: **Good Christian friends, rejoice with heart and
soul and voice!***

One: Rejoice that the members of our family will be getting
together this Christmas.

Rejoice that those in essential jobs and those who cannot
return home will be in contact through e-mail, texting,
Skype, and telephone.

Two: Rejoice that we will be sharing gifts and food with good
friends this Christmas time.

One: Rejoice that although the birth of Jesus Christ in lowly
isolation is in sharp contrast to the harsh light and loud
music of the commercial Christmas, we will hold Mary and
Joseph and the Christ Child in our hearts.

Young person: Rejoice! This is awesome!

Mother or Father: Rejoice! And thank God!

Grandparent or older person: Rejoice! And get busy!

*All sing: **Good Christian friends, rejoice with heart and
soul and voice!***

White Gift Sunday

A choral reading. This is an "eyes open" prayer of thanks for gifts to be shared in the local community after the service. *The gifts will vary from faith community to faith community, but the framework can remain.*

> We've got some gifts to share,
> We're very glad we're here.
> Some fun-full gifts,
> Some great toy gifts.

One: Like this car and these dolls.

Another: Like this Lego set and this front-end loader.

> For all these gifts,
> for those who will receive,
> we give God thanks.

> We've got some gifts to share,
> We're very glad we're here.
> Some useful gifts,
> Some practical gifts.

One: Like this set of cutlery.

Another: Like this scarf and mittens set.

> For all these gifts,
> for those who will receive,
> we give God thanks.

> We've got some gifts to share,
> We're very glad we're here.
> Some yummy gifts,
> Some mouthwatering gifts,

One: Like this voucher for a turkey.

Another: Like this iced Christmas cake.

> For all these gifts,
> for those who will receive,
> we give God thanks.

> We've got some gifts to share,
> We're very glad we're here.
> Some friendship gifts,
> some cheer up gifts.

One: Like this offer to share a handheld 20Q Harry Potter.
Another: Like this big hug for a friend who has been sick.
One: Like this potted chrysanthemum.
Another: Like this Christmas music CD.
For all these gifts,
for those who will receive,
we give God thanks.

All: **We've got some gifts to share,**
We're very glad we're here.
For all these gifts,
for those who will receive,
we give God thanks.
And we are very glad *you (choir points to*
congregation) **are here too! Amen.**

Advent 4

LECTIONARY READINGS
2 Samuel 7:1–11, 16
Luke 1:47–55 **or** Psalm 89:1–4, 19–26
Romans 16:25–27
Luke 1:26-38

Mary's song of praise.

One: We hear the voice of Mary.
All: My soul magnifies the Lord and my spirit rejoices in God my Saviour. God has brought down the powerful from their thrones, God has sent the rich empty away.
One: *(with increasing intensity)* If only! If only! If only!
If only the basic needs of children for shelter, adequate food, and medical care would be recognized and met worldwide.
If only the leaders of the powerful nations would have it in their hearts to share from their plenty!
If only the voices of those without adequate housing in our area would be heard!
If only the addicted ones would find acceptance and not rejection.
If only!
We hear the confident words of Mary.
All: My heart magnifies the Lord and my spirit rejoices in God my Saviour.

One: We hear the voice of Mary.
All: God has lifted up the lowly.
One: *(with increasing intensity)* One day it will happen! One day it will happen! One day it will happen!
One day it will happen! Depression and other mental health problems will be treated with the same priority and respect as physical problems.
One day it will happen! Those in hospitals and care homes without friends or family to advocate for them will get the same treatment as those who have a support system.

One day it will happen! The shy and those without self-confidence will have the courage to speak of the symptoms that worry them. We pray today for church members, friends, and family who are ill *(time of silent reflection)*.

One day it will happen! Those who suffer loss will find a sympathetic ear, and the bereaved will be able to express the anger and emptiness they feel *(time of silent reflection)*.

One day it will happen!

We hear the confident words of Mary.

All: My heart magnifies the Lord and my spirit rejoices in God my Saviour.

One We hear the voice of Mary.

All: Surely from now on all generations will be blessed.

One: *(with increasing intensity)* Are we sure? Are we sure? Are we sure?

Are we sure that the church will emerge from this uncertain time – this desert time – with zest and enthusiasm?

Are we sure that the church will be open to the forms of spirituality and music that are readily accepted by up coming generations?

Are we sure that the deeply held visions of clergy and congregants will be openly expressed and carefully heard?

Are we sure that the wisdom of other faith groups such as Buddhists and Muslims will find an arena of discussion alongside the teachings of Christianity?

We hear the confident words of Mary.

All: My heart magnifies the Lord and my spirit rejoices in God my Saviour.

One: We hear the voice of Mary.

All: The Mighty One has done great things for me.

One: *(with increasing intensity)* Can it be true? Can it be true? Can it be true?

Can it be true that we may praise God for the wonder and variety of creation?

Can it be true that such a diversity of talents and skills is ours to use and try?

Can it be true that we listen to the worries and fears of
our friends as readily as we speak of our own
concerns?
Can it be true that we have the courage to give voice to
our cherished dreams and put them into action?
We hear the confident words of Mary.
**All: My heart magnifies the Lord and my spirit rejoices
in God my Saviour.**

NOTE

The word magnifies may be replaced by praises.

Another Way

1. **The fourth Sunday in Advent is often celebrated as the Love
Sunday.**

We are amazed, O God, that you love the world so much:
A world torn by warfare and inter-racial strife,
A world of dramatic inequality and crying need,
A world where abuse and exploitation are commonplace *(time
of silent reflection).*
You love the world so much that you gave us Jesus,
and those who work in the spirit of your Chosen One.

*We are amazed, O God, that you love the suffering ones so
much:*
Those for whom sickness seems endless,
Those for whom there is no cure,
Those who wait for treatment,
Those who have suffered the loss of loved ones,
Those who have lost hope *(time of silent reflection).*
You love the suffering ones so much that you gave us Jesus,
**and those who work in the spirit of your Compassionate
One.**

We are amazed, O God, that you love your church so much:
A church warmly welcoming,
A church struggling to be faithful,

A church searching for a contemporary vision,
A church refusing to look only inward,
A church supporting the powerless and fearful *(time of silent reflection)*.
You love the church so much that you filled it with the spirit of Jesus,
and those who work in the spirit of your Anointed One.

We are amazed, O God, that you love each one of us so much:
In our times of selfishness and advantage seeking,
In our attitudes of self-doubt and inaction,
As we pay only lip service to Christian commitment,
As we see the dark places, yet refuse to bring the light *(time of silent reflection)*.
You love each one of us so much that you gave us the person of Jesus,
and the will to be faithful disciples.

2. Focus on thanksgiving for the gift of love.

Can we thank you enough, O God, for the gift of Jesus Christ?
We are amazed that you love the world so much:
A world torn by warfare and inter-racial strife,
A world of dramatic inequality and crying need,
A world where abuse and exploitation are commonplace.
You challenge the faithful to work for justice.
You love the world so much that you gave us Jesus,
and are beside those who work in the spirit of your Chosen One.

Can we thank you enough, O God, for the gift of Jesus Christ?
We are amazed, O God, that you love the suffering ones so much:
Those for whom sickness seems endless,
Those for whom there is no cure,
Those who wait for treatment,
Those who have suffered the loss of loved ones,

Those who have lost hope *(time of silent reflection)*.
There are no limits to your call for compassion, God.
You love the world so much that you gave us Jesus,
and are beside those who work in the spirit of your
Chosen One.

Can we thank you enough, O God, for the gift of Jesus
Christ?
We are amazed, O God, that you love your church so much:
A church warmly welcoming,
A church struggling to be faithful,
A church searching for a contemporary vision,
A church refusing to look only inward,
A church supporting the powerless and fearful.
You refuse to let us look only inwards.
You love the world so much that you gave us Jesus,
and are beside those who work in the spirit of your
Chosen One.

Can we thank you enough, O God, for the gift of Jesus
Christ?
We are amazed, O God, that you love each one of us so much:
In our times of selfishness and advantage seeking,
In our attitudes of self-doubt and inaction,
As we pay lip service to Christian commitment,
As we see the dark places yet refuse to bring the light.
But you see the best in us and encourage our faithfulness.
You love each one of us so much that you gave us Jesus,
and are beside us as we work in the spirit of your
Chosen One.

3. Turn this into a prayer of questioning.

We thank you, O God, for the gift of Jesus Christ.
We are amazed, O God, that you love our church so much.
We rejoice that you are with us as our church is a leader in
    mission.
But how can you love us when our congregation is
preoccupied with our own small concerns?
We rejoice that you are with us when the church takes
    initiatives in worship and serving the local community.

But how can you love us when we will not accept a faithful vision?
We rejoice that you are with us when we practice justice and inclusion.
But how can you love us when we avoid the issues, and give a half-hearted welcome?
You love the world so much that you gave us Jesus,
and are beside those who work in the spirit of your Chosen One.

We thank you, O God, for the gift of Jesus Christ.

We are amazed that you love each one of us so much.
We rejoice that you love us when we help and support.
But how can you love us when we are selfish and seek to take advantage?
We rejoice that you love us when we take the initiative and lead.
But how can you love us when we doubt our abilities and hang back?
We rejoice that you love us when we serve faithfully.
But how can you love us when we pay only lip service to our Christian commitment?
You love each one of us so much that you gave us Jesus,
and are beside us as we work in the spirit of your Chosen One.

Follow the same pattern for the other sections.

---

4. Instead of using the response, My heart magnifies…, the congregation might sing the refrain of *My Soul Cries Out* (*More Voices* #120).

SEASON OF CHRISTMAS
Christmas Eve/Day
Christmas, Proper 1 (Years A, B, C)

LECTIONARY READINGS
Isaiah 9:2–7
Psalm 96
Titus 2:11–14
Luke 2:1–14, (15–20)

*The traditional story of the first Christmas: Mary, Joseph,
the angels, and the shepherds.*

**Mary and Joseph arrive at Bethlehem. Mary is expecting
a baby.**
This is a story that brings us to prayer.
We pray for loved ones who are travelling, and remember
those who have no close family or friends.
We pray for refugees far from their homeland: women at risk,
frightened children, and men who are homesick.
We pray for *(insert own words)*.
And we pray for people who are separated from their families
because they work today: aircrew and innkeepers, hydro
repair gangs, and drivers who transport food.
As we pray the questions come to us:
**How can we help? How can we support? How can we be
in touch?**

**Mary and Joseph cannot find even the shelter of an inn for
the birth, so Mary has her baby in a stable. It's a boy.**
This is a story that brings us to prayer.
We pray for women who are pregnant.
We pray for couples who cannot have children.
We pray for those who worry about the health of their
children, and those whose Christmas joy is overshadowed
because they are sick.
We think of those who are in hospital and wish they were
home celebrating.
We bring those we know before you, Holy One *(time of silent
reflection)*.

We remember those who have lost loved ones; past family
gatherings and shared Christmas meals come to mind.
We bring those we know before you, Holy One *(time of silent
reflection).*
As we pray the questions come to us:
**How can we help? How can we support? How can we be
in touch?**

*The shepherds encounter an angel who tells them to put
their fear aside.*
*The sky is filled with an angel choir singing, "Glory to
God in highest heaven."*
This is a story that brings us to prayer.
We pray for those we know who cannot conquer their fears,
and those affected by unforeseen and troubling experiences.
We give thanks for this service of worship: the carols, prayers,
and readings.
We give thanks for all the joy, inspiration, and compassionate
opportunities that are ours in faith community.
We pray for those who lead and guide our faith community,
and for those of our church family who are in the midst of
tough and challenging times *(time of silent reflection).*
As we pray, the questions come to us:
**How can we help? How can we support? How can we be
in touch?**

*The shepherds rush down the hillside to visit Mary and
Joseph and report what the angel told them about their
newborn son. They hurry off to spread the good news.*
This is a story that brings us to prayer.
It reminds us of new friends.
It reminds us of the joyful celebrations we take part in at this
festive time.
It reminds us of the good news that we have heard over this
Advent and Christmas time: good family news, and happy
world happenings, such as *(current event).*
It is a story that challenges us to look at the positive and
encouraging events in our lives.
It is a story that takes us into the New Year with hope.

It is a story that reminds us to thank God
for those who have helped us, those who have
supported us, and those who have been in touch at
this wonder-full time of year.

Another Way

1. Sing the first part of *Glory to God* (*More Voices* #36) after each
   of the first three prayer sections and sing the "Alleluia Amen"
   at the end of the prayer. Or sing *Gloria* (*Voices United* #37)
   after each section of the prayer.

2. Use a more concise prayer.

Bring a new world to birth, O God.
Silence the guns of the aggressors, transform the hate of the
   terrorists, give warmth and security to the homeless.
Bring the bond of human affection to those who lack love.
Encourage us to act as midwives to bring about peace, end
   alienation, and create safe places for the fearful.
The birth of Jesus
opens up new possibilities.

Bring a compassionate society to birth, O God.
Be a hope-giving presence to the sick.
Aid the harassed caregivers.
Comfort those who mourn.
Hear the frustration of those on strike or without work.
Encourage us to act as midwives to bring about support,
   perspective, and deep listening *(time of silent reflection)*.
The birth of Jesus
opens up new possibilities.

Bring a renewed church to birth, O God.
Ready this faith community for outreach.
Encourage those who are downhearted.
Foster cooperation with other faith communities, churches,
   and denominations.

Promote a spirit of generosity among those who give for
mission.
Encourage us to act as midwives to bring about enthusiasm,
flexibility, and liberality.
The birth of Jesus
opens up new possibilities.

Bring each one of us to a new beginning, O God.
Refuse to accept our self-imposed limitations.
Affirm our worth in the eyes of others.
Enable us to be done with apathy.
Help us to put depression behind us.
Show us how we can live our dreams.
Encourage us to see you as Holy Midwife birthing us to our
Christian potential.
The birth of Jesus
opens up new possibilities.

3. **Use the phrase "a new beginning" throughout the prayer.**

A new beginning:
Each and every sick person is supported.
A new beginning:
Caregivers are noticed and helped.
A new beginning:
The bereaved are comforted *(time of silent reflection)*.
A new beginning:
Those on strike or without work find a listening ear.
Encourage us to act as midwives to bring support, perspective,
and a listening ear.
The birth of Jesus
opens up new possibilities.

A new beginning:
This faith community renews its engagement with the local
community.
A new beginning:
Those who are downhearted are identified and affirmed.

A new beginning:
Faith groups are contacted *(insert the names of local groups, such as Buddhists, Hindus)*.
Local *(same denomination)* churches are contacted *(insert the name of the denomination)*.
Local *(different denomination)* churches are contacted *(insert the name of church)*.
A new beginning:
Those who give for mission find a new spirit of generosity.
Encourage us to act as midwives to bring about enthusiasm, flexibility, and liberality.
The birth of Jesus
opens up new possibilities.

Christmas Day/Eve
Proper 2 (A, B, C)

LECTIONARY READINGS
Isaiah 62:6–12
Psalm 97
Titus 3:4–7
Luke 2:(1–7), 8–20

The visit of the shepherds and the response of Mary.

**In that region there were shepherds watching over their
flocks.**
Careful and diligent shepherds, call us to remember the good
    leaders of our time and place:
Leaders who speak out for those least able to speak for
    themselves;
Leaders willing to take hard decisions so that the world will be
    a healthy and safe place
    for our children and grandchildren;
Leaders who refuse to use their position for personal profit or
    advantage;
Leaders who take the time to consult with ordinary people
    before acting.
**Glory to God in highest heaven,
and on earth, peace.**

**The shepherds said, "Let us go to Bethlehem and see this
thing that has taken place."**
Shepherds who are ready to find out for themselves what has
    happened call us to remember our need to get involved:
To be concerned for individuals alone or far from home who
    wish they had someone to be with;
To be concerned for families for whom Christmas is a time
    that bitterly emphasizes how little they have in comparison
    with others;
To visit and care for those who are confined to home or a
    hospital bed;

To support and listen to those whose feelings are intense at
this time of year because they have lost a loved one *(time of
silent reflection).*
Glory to God in highest heaven,
and on earth, peace.

**The shepherds found Mary and Joseph and the child lying
in the manger. They made known what they had been
told about the child. And everyone was amazed at what
the shepherds had told them.**
The shepherds had an amazing story to tell. It was a story
with good news at the heart of it.
We thank God for opportunities to share the good news about
the birth of Jesus in our own church and neighbourhood.
We thank God for the opportunities to share worship, praise,
and carol singing with other churches in our locality.
We thank God for the opportunity to share our Christmas joy
with those who are housebound or in care homes.
We thank God for the opportunity to give gifts of food,
clothes, and money to those in our neighbourhood who
need a helping hand.
Glory to God in highest heaven,
and on earth, peace.

**Mary treasured all these words and pondered them in her
heart.**
The age-old story has touched us again this Christmas. It has
renewed our faith and called us to action. Why are we so
surprised?
We hear of a young couple far from home, lacking
accommodation, and we realize we have couples like that in
(our own town/city).
We think of the loneliness of Mary and Joseph, and we recall
our own experiences of loneliness and fear.
We hear of Mary treasuring wonderful holy experiences and
we think back to times when we have been moved to the
depths of our being by the words, sounds, and signs of God.
And we feel ready to join the angel choir as they sing,
Glory to God in highest heaven,
and on earth, peace.

Another Way

1. Sing *Come Now, O God of Peace* (*Voices United* #34) at the end of each prayer section in place of the last two lines.

2. Use contemporary Christmas events and items as a theme. An "eyes open" prayer.

Have food items such as Christmas baking and chocolates displayed on the Communion table.

The smell of foods cooking at Christmas calls us to eat and pray.
For good food and the farmers who produce it,
we thank you, God.
For those who provide food for the hungry, like *(local food bank, shelter)*,
we thank you, God.
For those who develop efficient means of cultivation, and those who responsibly tread the path of organic farming,
we thank you, God.
For those who have different Christmas food traditions,
For those who love to eat vegetables or fish and for those who grow and harvest these foods,
we thank you, God.
A (mouthwatering) time of reflection.

Display Christmas cards, phone cards, and family pictures on the Communion table.

Phone calls and emails from those far away call us to prayer.
For loved ones and family members far from here,
Loving God, we pray.
For those who have to work and cannot have Christmas off – Hydro repair persons, hotel staff, and those who work for airlines or taxi companies,
Loving God, we pray.
For staff in care homes and hospitals, and for the residents and patients who dearly wish they could be in their own homes,

Loving God, we thank you.
(A time of reflection.)

A cross and candle will already be on the Communion table; add a nativity scene or church school/youth group craft.

 In the familiar carols and songs, and the glowing decorations
    of Advent and Christmas,
we rejoice, Loving God.
In the worship of those who join us at this festival time,
we rejoice, Loving God.
In the opportunity to give to mission funds and to local food
    and shelter groups,
we rejoice, Loving God.

A congregational family could come and stand in front of the Communion table.

 For the joy of family and friends around us,
we praise you, God.
For the break from the daily work routine,
we praise you, God.
For contact with those who are at a distance, yet whose love is
    present with us,
we praise you, God

Alternatively, the family members at the front of the church could ask members of the congregation to say what they are especially grateful for. The offered thanksgivings could then be incorporated into a series of prayer phrases used in a prayer like the one above.

Christmas Day/Eve
Proper 3 (A, B, C)

LECTIONARY READINGS
Isaiah 52:7–10
Psalm 98
Hebrews1:1–4, (5–12)
John 1:1–14

*The true light that enlightens everyone was coming
into the world.*

Give us your light, God.
The light of peace in the midst of conflict *(current event/s)*.
The light of sharing in the midst of hunger *(current situation)*.
The light of new learning in the midst of old skills and
   practices.
The light of simplicity in our complex and challenging world.
Give us your light, God,
the light we know in Jesus the Christ.

Give us your light, God.
The light of listening to the old and infirm.
The light of empathy for the deeply troubled.
The light of direct speaking to those who would bully and
   manipulate.
The light of a quiet friendship with those who are sick or in
   pain *(time of silent reflection)*.
The light of support and presence to those who have lost loved
   ones *(time of silent reflection)*.
Give us your light, God,
the light we know in Jesus the Christ.

Give us your light, God.
The joyful light that we experience in prayer and worship.
The affirming light that we know as faith community.
The practical light that we work out of as we share gifts and
   time with the troubled and afraid.
The everlasting light that accompanies us through life and
   beyond.
Give us your light, God,
the light we know in Jesus the Christ.

Give us your light, God.
The light that shows us talents and skills that we are
    unaware of.
The light of truth that enables us to see people and situations
    differently.
The light that changes our priorities.
The light that endures rejection.
The light that enables us to follow faithfully, yet question
    directly.
The light that endures the darkest moment of the darkest day.
The light that is not diminished by the end of our time.
Give us your light, God,
the light we know in Jesus the Christ.

Another Way

1. Have a different member of the congregation light a tealight
   as each line of the prayer is offered.

2. A Prayer of Thanksgiving and Concern

Thank you, O God, for your goodness to our world at this
    Coming of Jesus *time.*
Thank you for those who are working for peace.
Thank you for agencies feeding the hungry.
Thank you for the powerless who encourage other powerless
    ones.
We pray for the rejected and those who are victims of
    injustice.
We pray for people who cannot find a warm place to sleep.
We pray for prisoners denied helpful insight and the
    opportunity to change, and we pray for political prisoners.
We pray for those separated by distance or anger.
May our speaking out and practical help
be a sign of your Blessed One
come at Christmastime.

Thank you, O God, for the blessings of this **Coming of Jesus** *time.*
Thank you for the return of family members.
Thank you for messages from loved ones far away.
Thank you for the visits of friends.
Thank you for the good smells of festive food cooking and
mysterious presents round the tree.
**And we pray for those for whom Christmas is a
challenging time.**
We pray for people who live alone and have few friends.
We pray for those who cannot afford Christmas food or gifts.
We pray for families where there is quarrelling *(time of silent
reflection)*.
May our sharing and acceptance
be a sign of your Blessed One
come at Christmastime.

 Thank you, O God, for the blessings of this **Coming of Jesus** *time.*
Thank you for good health and for the blessing of health
restored.
Thank you for satisfying work and social gatherings filled
with chat and laughter.
Thank you for the ability to walk or run or turn cartwheels.
Thank you for the opportunity to meditate or pray or reflect
(time of silent reflection).
**We pray for those who feel downhearted, for patients
who are not getting better, for those who have to work
over the holiday.**
We pray for faithful members who cannot come to church.
We pray for people who miss loved ones so much *(time of
silent reflection)*.
May our understanding and support,
be a sign of your Blessed One
come at Christmastime

3. Sing the first verse of *We Give Our Thanks to God* (*More
   Voices* #187) after each section, or after the times of silent
   reflection in the prayer.

1st Sunday after Christmas

LECTIONARY READINGS
Isaiah 61:10—62:3
Psalm 148
Galatians 4:4–7
Luke 2:22–40

Simeon recognizes the worth of God's chosen child.

Give thanks for God's chosen child, Jesus.
A sign from God that the powerful cannot forever subdue the
weak *(relate a national or international event)*.
A sign from God that the worth of children will be recognized
and the wisdom of elders respected.
A sign from God that the environment will be protected and
birds, fish, and wild animals will have secure habitat *(relate
to national or international stories or agencies)*.
A sign from God that warfare will cease and the women and
men of peace will be heard *(relate a national or
international event)*.
In our thanksgiving for the Christ child,
there is hope without limit.

Give thanks for God's chosen child, Jesus.
A sign from God that the paid or voluntary work of each
person will be appreciated.
A sign from God that the challenged and struggling will not be
forgotten.
A sign from God that the discouraged will be supported.
A sign from God that those sick in mind or body will be
lovingly treated *(time of silent reflection)*.
A sign from God that the bereaved will be given their grieving
time *(time of silent reflection)*.
In our thanksgiving for the Christ child,
there is hope without limit.

Give thanks for God's chosen child, Jesus.
A sign from God that church will be freed from outdated
traditions.

A sign from God that faith community members will appreciate the gifts of each other.

A sign from God that the careful leadership within our church, both lay and clergy, *(mention specific names)* will be cherished and thanked.

A sign from God enshrined in good words in the Bible.

A sign from God that the church can go joyfully into a new year.

In our thanksgiving for the Christ child,
there is hope without limit.

Give thanks for God's chosen child, Jesus.
Our sign from God that we will never be alone in time or space.

Our sign from God that the past no longer has power over us.

Our sign from God that we are able to choose fresh opportunities and directions.

Our sign from God that our abilities and resources are greater than we acknowledge.

Our sign from God that there are no limits to God's love for us.

In our thanksgiving for the Christ child,
there is hope without limit.

Another Way

1. **After each section sing** *Jesus Came Bringing Us Hope (love/joy/ peace)* **(***More Voices* **#33).**

2. **Base the prayer on Luke 2:40, The child grew and God's blessings were on him.**

In the Christ child we are blessed.
God's saving grace for the world is revealed.

Just and saving God, you are there when God's prophets and wise ones speak out fearlessly and work tirelessly. We think of *(mention by name contemporary saints and statespersons)*.

Just and saving God, you are there when those who exploit

women and children for selfish gain are exposed.
Just and saving God, you are there when persons challenged
in body and mind are encouraged in their areas of ability.
Just and saving God, you are there when prisoners are
affirmed for the fulfilled and productive men and women
they will become.
Just and saving God, you are there when those denied jobs
or accommodation because of their racial origin or facial
characteristics have their rights recognized.
Jesus grew, became strong, and was full of wisdom.
We rejoice that we follow God's Blessed One.

In the Christ child we are blessed.
God's saving grace for the suffering ones is revealed.
Passionate God, you will not rest until those denied work find
opportunities to match their capabilities.
Passionate God, you will not rest until the old and infirm
receive the same attention as the younger and more
articulate.
Passionate God, you will not rest until those who endure
constant and peace-denying pain find relief.
Passionate God, you will not rest until those conditions that
sap the life-spirit of young boys and girls *(such as...)* are
researched and overcome.
Passionate God, you will not rest until those who have
lost loved ones find a supportive presence to share their
emptiness *(time of silent reflection)*.
Jesus grew, became strong, and was full of wisdom.
We rejoice that we follow God's Blessed One.

In the Christ child we are blessed.
God's saving grace for the church is revealed.
God of the church, you stay with us in the dry and wandering
times. You are faithful when we are not.
God of the church, you stay with us as we struggle to break
from the old creeds and patterns and learn new ways.
God of the church, you are with us as we vision and dream of
a faithful future. You keep us on task.
God of the church, you stay with us in the valley of the
shadow. Always you stay with us, always.
Jesus grew, became strong, and was full of wisdom.
We rejoice that we follow God's Blessed One.

In the Christ child we are blessed.
God's saving grace for each one of us is revealed.
Loving God, you are with us on those dark days whether we
sense your presence or not.
Loving God, you are with us as we celebrate and rejoice.
   When we find a new job, or have a new child or grandchild,
   or meet an old friend after a long absence, you are there in
   our laughter and tears of joy.
Loving God, you go with us when the way ahead is uncertain
   and testing.
You are there as we search out a fresh career path or area of
   voluntary service.
You are there giving us the confidence to venture out, and you
   are there calling us to patience.
Loving God, you are there as we search for and find our
   spiritual direction.
Jesus grew, became strong, and was full of wisdom.
We rejoice that we follow God's Blessed One.

New Year's Day or Sunday

LECTIONARY READINGS
Ecclesiastes 3:1–13
Psalm 8
Revelation 21:1–6a
Matthew 25:31–46

Ecclesiastes: There is a time for everything.
Matthew: Be ready, the Son of Man comes when
you least expect him.

Are you ready for the New Year?
We are ready!
We celebrate the opportunities a new year brings:
The chance to become a part of the political process.
The chance to become involved in the struggles of the
   powerless;
The chance to look at our planet with the eyes of our
   grandchildren and their children;
The chance to take on board the huge gap between rich and
   poor nations and advocate for change;
The chance to offer practical help to one group or family in
   our community.
We celebrate the opportunity a new year brings.
We are ready,
and we will go to work joyfully.

Are you ready for the New Year?
We are ready!
We celebrate the opportunities a new year brings:
The prospect of fresh training and job possibilities for those
   frustrated in job search;
The prospect of more chances for men as teachers and for
   women as business leaders;
The prospect of relief from pain for those chronically ill;
The prospect of diagnosis or healing for those who we know
   among the suffering in our family and our church family
   (time of silent reflection);
The prospect of new strength and hope for the bereaved.

Who can we stand beside? Who can we support?
We celebrate the opportunities a new year brings.
We are ready,
and we will go to work joyfully.

Are you ready for the New Year?
We are ready!
We celebrate the opportunities a new year brings:
A time for fresh visioning for our church *(specific initiatives could be mentioned);*
A time for learning about our faith and studying the Bible;
A time for rededicating ourselves to the mission of our denomination;
A time for reaching out to other faiths and Christian partners in our area.
We celebrate the opportunities a new year brings.
We are ready,
and we will go to work joyfully.

Are you ready for the New Year?
We are ready!
There are those with whom we would be friends.
There are previous habits and relationships that we want to put behind us.
There are new ventures in our work and social groups that we want to be about.
There are past grudges we want to be rid of.
There are dreams we want to bring to reality.
There is spiritual life that we want to revive.
We celebrate the opportunities a new year brings.
We are ready,
and we will go to work joyfully.

Another Way

1. **Use the above prayer as the outline and pose (and answer) the question, "In whom will we see Jesus in the new year?"**

In whom will we see Jesus in the new year?
We will see Jesus in the struggles of the powerless.

We will see Jesus though the perceptive eyes of the next
generations.
We will see Jesus among those who advocate for reducing the
huge gap between rich and poor.
We will see Jesus as we offer practical help to one group or
family in our neighbourhood.
We celebrate the opportunities a new year brings.
We are ready,
and we will go to work joyfully.

In whom will we see Jesus in the new year?
We will see Jesus as those frustrated in the job search find
fresh training and job prospects.
We will see Jesus in men who become teachers and women
who become leaders in business.
We will see Jesus in persons who relieve the pain of those who
suffer terribly.
We will see Jesus in those who take the necessary time to
diagnose and treat illness *(time of silent reflection).*
We will see Jesus among those who bring new strength and
hope to the bereaved.
Who can we stand beside? Who can we support?
We celebrate the opportunities a new year brings.
We are ready,
and we will go to work joyfully.

---

2. **Base the prayer on Ecclesiastes, There is a time for everything.**

In step with God, there is a time for everything:
A time for affirming our political leaders in their actions, and
a time to call them to account.
A time for speaking out for the poorest and oppressed, and a
time to work with them.
A time for rejoicing in our national heritage and traditions,
and a time to support the ways of newcomers to our nation.
A time for standing alongside those who are this nation's first
peoples, and a time to support their aspirations for basic
services, for land, and for respect.
As the new year unfolds,
we will work in God's good time.

In step with God, there is a time for everything:
A time for trying out a new medication, and a time to rely on
trusted drugs.
A time for carefully following the advice of your physician,
and a time to ask for a second opinion.
A time for closely supporting a family member or friend who
is sick, and a time to stand back and let them take necessary
decisions.
We remember those of our own family and our church family
who are sick *(time of silent reflection)*.
A time for listening carefully to those who have lost a loved
one, and a time to encourage them to find a group of
bereaved persons.
As the new year unfolds,
we will work in God's good time.

In step with God, there is a time for everything.
A time for trying new church ventures, and a time to rejoice
in the present pattern of worship and service;
A time for thanking and encouraging leaders and teachers
of the faith community, and a time to assess their work
performance.
A time for stressing the needs of the local congregation, and a
time to speak out for the needs of our mission partners.
As the new year unfolds,
we will work in God's good time.

In step with God, there is a time for everything:
A time for stepping out in new directions, a time for seeing
the worth of traditional ways. A time for giving thanks for
the familiar routine, a time for letting go of ways that are
negative and stale.
A time for challenging those who would put us down, and a
time for seeking forgiveness from those we have hurt and
ignored.
A time for valuing friendships and family ties, a time for
making new friends and putting unhealthy relationships
behind us.
As the new year unfolds,
we will work in God's good time.

SEASON AFTER THE EPIPHANY
Epiphany of the Lord

LECTIONARY READINGS
Isaiah 60:1–6
Psalm 72:1–7,10–14
Ephesians 3:1–12
Matthew 2:1–12

The magi follow the star and find the holy family.

The star is ahead of us – the promise of hope reborn.
The star of peace in the midst of earth's troubled places *(detail current troubled countries).*
The star of opportunity for those seeking work in our area.
The star of freedom for those who are bound by unhealthy relationships.
The star of affirmation for those who cannot believe in themselves.
Hope reborn through the efforts of men and women who share a common humanity.
The star is ahead of us.
We follow the star.

The star is ahead of us – the promise of healing.
The promise of care for those who await placement in a senior's residence.
The promise of respite for those who are worn out with caregiving.
The promise of patience for those in the surgery line-up.
The promise of a better day for those who are slow to heal.
The promise of a sympathetic listener for those who are afraid of voicing their deepest fears *(time of silent reflection).*
The promise of peace for those going through the valley of the shadow.
The promise of comfort for those who have lost loved ones *(time of silent reflection).*
The promise of healing in the midst of suffering and loss.
The star is ahead of us.
We follow the star.

The star is ahead of us – shining on the way to a faithful church.
Enlightening us as we seek the ties that bind us in the love of Christ.
Enlightening us as we strive to look beyond our church walls to those in need on the streets of our town.
Challenging us to widen our horizons so that our care extends to those countries and areas that the mission fund supports.
The star points to a faith community where we do together what we cannot possibly do on our own.
The star is ahead of us.
We follow the star.

The star is ahead of us – lighting up our own faith journey.
Helping us to see our doubts as stepping stones on the way to a rooted faith.
Giving us the security we need when our supports fall away.
Providing a focus when we feel the call to venture out unafraid.
Enabling us to put our carelessness and self-doubts behind us.
The star finds its resting place where the love of God in Jesus shines out.
The star is ahead of us.
We follow the star.

Another Way

1. Focus on light in the darkness.

The light of Jesus Christ comes into the darkness of the world.
Into the hard place of the prison cell comes the light of new insight and hope.
Into the village where women have to walk miles to get fresh water comes the gift of a simple water pump.
Into the home where one parent juggles a full-time job with care for young children comes the support of family, friends, or a nurturing daycare person.
Into the business where workers feel stress comes the gentle

organizer with the ability to suggest changes that bring
clarity.
We will be light bringers.
**We will support the light bringers in the way of Jesus
Christ.**

*The light of Jesus Christ comes into the dark place of
suffering.*
Where health professionals struggle to diagnose, there is
persistence.
Where memory loss increases, there is a readiness to face the
new reality.
Where children experience pain, there is quiet understanding.
We silently remember those of our own family, our friends, and
our church family who are going through tough times today
(time of silent reflection).
Where loneliness has become a nagging pain, there is a reaching
out to groups of friendly people.
Where a loved one has died, there is time to come to terms with
loss, and to grieve.
We will be light bringers.
**We will support the light bringers in the way of Jesus
Christ.**

*The light of Jesus Christ comes into the dark places of the
church.*
With fresh images of God comes an opening of minds.
Where there is a divide between age groups come initiatives to
bring common ground and understanding.
Where there is resistance to serving the spiritual needs of those
outside the church comes renewed empathy and enthusiasm.
Where there is reluctance to give for the work of the wider
church comes a new appreciation of what mission work is
about.
We will be light bringers.
**We will support the light bringers in the way of Jesus
Christ.**

*The light of Jesus Christ comes into the dark places of our
own lives.*
When we lack the will to take a decision, we summon the
courage to move forward.

When we are troubled by a breakdown in relationship, we
    search out the cause and work to restore good feelings.
When we know that apathy and uncaring have a hold on us,
    we work to become focused and empathetic again.
When we hold a grudge against a person close to us, we
    acknowledge feelings and bring a change of heart.
**We *are* the light bringers of Jesus Christ, and we need
the light of Christ in our own lives.**

---

2. Use the theme of starlight in a shorter prayer

Rays of Starlight
Prisoners find ways to live useful lives and have peace.
Hard pressed women in Africa get micro-loans that enable
    them to start a business.
Employers provide daycare for the children of working
    mothers and fathers.
The local authority supports programs for older persons with
    mobility problems and learning needs.
We can be a source of starlight.
We can advocate and work for change.

Rays of starlight.
Fresh ways of describing and experiencing God.
The generations eating and studying together.
New songs that touch the hearts of the whole congregation.
Programs and groups that are geared to those outside church
    membership.
We can be a source of starlight.
We can advocate and work for change.

Follow the same pattern for the other sections.

**3. Sing *Jesus Came Bringing Us Hope* (*More Voices* #33) after
each section, but substitute the word light for "hope" "peace"
or "joy." Or sing the refrain of *I Am the Light of the World*
(*Voices United* #87) at the end of each section.**

1st Sunday after the Epiphany

(Baptism of Jesus)

LECTIONARY READINGS

Genesis 1:1–5
Psalm 29
Acts 19:1–7
Mark 1:4–11

The baptism of Jesus by John.

***John's baptism led to a new life for Jesus. New life is God's
promise for people worldwide.***
The poor recognized, encouraged, and supported. We pray for
(local initiative).
The domination by the economically strong no longer
acceptable. We pray for *(instance of international
domination)*.
Discrimination on the grounds of racial origin at an end *(local
example)*.
Conflicts between nations ended through peaceful negotiation.
We pray for *(international situation)*.
**We the baptized
will nurture and encourage new life.**

***John's baptism led to a new life for Jesus. New life is God's
promise for suffering people.***
The determination to face the reality of financial troubles.
A will to persist after months or years without work.
The ability to cope while balancing home and work
responsibilities.
A sense of hope during an illness that goes on and on.
Deep peace for those who are dying, and a thorough time of
grieving for the bereaved *(time of silent reflection)*.
**We the baptized
will nurture and encourage new life.**

***John's baptism led to a new life for Jesus. New life is God's
promise for the faith community.***
Newcomers welcomed joyfully and sensitively.
Community groups initiated and supported. We pray for
(groups are named).

The oldest and the youngest respected and listened to.
Church leaders acknowledged and thanked wholeheartedly.
Local and overseas mission treated as essential.
We the baptized
will nurture and encourage new life.

John's baptism led to a new life for Jesus. New life is God's
promise for each one of us.
Caution before we rush into uncertain ventures.
Calm amid life's struggles.
Determination when apathy saps our will to act.
Perseverance in the face of obstacles and problems.
Joy within the humdrum of daily life.
Fearless faith when facing the challenges of life.
We have been baptized,
and we will experience the new life God offers us.

Another Way

1. **At the front of the worship area, ladle or pour water from one container into another after each phrase of the prayer.**

John's baptism led to a new life for Jesus. New life is God's
promise for the faith community.
Newcomers welcomed joyfully and sensitively *(water poured,*
brief time of reflection).
The oldest and the youngest respected and supported *(water*
poured, brief time of reflection).
Church leaders acknowledged and thanked wholeheartedly
(water poured, brief time of reflection).
Local and overseas mission treated as essential *(water poured,*
brief time of reflection).
We the baptized
will nurture and encourage new life.

Follow the same pattern for the other sections.

2. **Sing a verse of a baptismal song or hymn after each section of the prayer.** *Behold, Behold, I Make All Things New* (*More Voices* #115) **is especially appropriate.**

2nd Sunday after the Epiphany

LECTIONARY READINGS
1 Samuel 3:1–10, (11–20)
Psalm 139:1–6,13–18
1 Corinthians 6:12–20
John 1:43–51

*Phillip recognizes Jesus as God's promised one and
tells Nathaniel about him. Both become disciples.*

 *You see us clearly, Graceful God, and you call us to
recognize the needy of our world.*
The despair of the homeless.
The fatigue of the overworked.
The despair of the prisoners.
The frustration of the illiterate.
The heartache of the powerless.
The loneliness of the friendless.
And you ask us to ask ourselves,
Have I a role to play in meeting their needs?

 *You see us clearly, Graceful God, and you call us to
recognize the needy in our neighbourhood.*
The anguish of those who cannot control their gambling habit.
The desperation of those who cannot control their spending.
The frustration of those who have to wait for medical care.
The frustration of persons who increasingly lose their
    mobility.
The sadness of those estranged from family and friends.
The hopelessness of the bereaved *(time of silent reflection)*.
And you ask us to ask ourselves,
Have I a role to play in meeting their needs?

 *You see us clearly, Graceful God, and you call us to
recognize the needs found in our church.*
The need for fresh, energetic leadership in the local
    congregation. We think of *(specify the areas of need)*.
The spiritual needs of non-churchgoers.
Helping disadvantaged persons in partnership with
    community resources. We think of *(specify the areas of need)*.

Vital mission projects as well as local ones.
And you ask us to ask ourselves,
Have I a role to play in meeting those needs?

 You see us clearly, Graceful God, and you call us to
    recognize the needs that are ours alone.
Being ready to put past mistakes and troubles behind us.
Believing we have been forgiven.
Making an agonizing difficult decision.
Saying the words that need to be said.
Taking action not just talking.
Helping a friend in trouble.
Facing up to our most threatening situations.
And you alert us to your sustaining presence at our
    most crucial times.
Amen.

Another Way

1. Focus the prayer on the theme of "response to call." This
    theme is in both the Christian and Hebrew scriptures for today.

 We listen for your call, O God:
    From persons who do not know where the next meal is
        coming from;
    From young persons whose pleas for attention and help go
        unheard;
    From those who lack the resources to follow their chosen
        vocation;
    From a family member in trouble.
    We listen for your call, O God, and our response is
        straightforward:
    Speak, your servant is listening.

 We listen for your call, O God:
    From those who are wrecked on the financial rocks;
    From those who will not heed the advice of therapists or
        medical personnel;
    From those who have lost the will to respond and take action;

From those for whom life seems unbearable;
From those who are close to life's end;
From those who are in the deep well of bereavement *(time of silent reflection).*
We listen for your call, O God, and our response is straightforward:
Speak, your servant is listening.

Follow the same pattern for the other sections.

2. Sing a verse of a hymn or song with "call" as a theme after each section of the prayer. For example, verse one of *Jesus Calls Us* (*Voices United* #562), or *Will You Come and Follow Me* (*Voices United* #567) or *Listen, God Is Calling* (*More Voices* #97).

3rd Sunday after the Epiphany

LECTIONARY READINGS

Jonah 3:1–5, 10
Psalm 62:5–12
1 Corinthians 7:29–31
Mark 1:14–20

Becoming a friend of Jesus and obedience to the call are the themes of the Christian scriptures.

It is your friendship we seek, O God, for it is constant, unchanging, empathetic, and to be trusted totally. We seek it for our world, for our church, for those (known and unknown to us) who are suffering; we seek it for ourselves.

When we recognize your friendship at work in the world, O God, we understand how great changes have small beginnings.
New understanding comes to our support of refugees when we hear of women without any protection in refugee camps.
A renewed urgency to provide low-cost housing comes when we hear of lives lost through fires in sub-standard homes.
A sense of what it is to be unemployed arises from hearing the troubling account of a person who can't find work.
The will to help the hungry comes from the encounter with one desperately needy person.
As friends of Jesus,
we will respond practically, appropriately, and compassionately.

When we recognize your friendship at work among the suffering, O God, we understand how the health professional and the visitor both have a part to play.
Tender touch enables patients in hospital to feel that their needs matter to staff members.
Your intently listening ear enables the deepest feelings of those going through hard times to be heard.
A quiet presence – steady, reassuring, and never failing – is simply there for those who suffer.

Strong support comforts those who are going through the
valley of the shadow.
We pray for those who are known and loved, especially those
in our own and church families. We pray for our friends
(time of silent reflection).
As friends of Jesus,
**we will respond practically, appropriately, and
compassionately.**

*When we recognize your friendship at work within the
church, O God, we understand how strength and growth
may come.*
Eyes open to the stranger and newcomer, making them
welcome, inviting them in.
Your creative Spirit working in new ways, singing a new song,
challenging old practices.
A broadness of mind and heart that lets us see beyond the
usual.
A perceptive awareness that recognizes skills and gifts not yet
used for the faith community.
In silence we reflect on the needs of the local and wider
church.
As friends of Jesus,
**we will respond practically, appropriately, and
compassionately.**

*When we recognize your friendship at work within each
one of us, we understand how far your love goes.*
Steering us gently in directions that are helpful, fulfilling, and
selfless.
Challenging us relentlessly to wake up to the attitudes,
prejudices, and practices that we know to be wrong.
Nurturing our offers of companionship and service to others
when it is easier to go it alone.
Understanding your never failing acceptance of each of us, no
matter how far we stray from you.
*We are deeply grateful to be counted as present-day
friends of Jesus.*
**Our service of Jesus will be practical, appropriate, and
compassionate.**

Another Way

---

1. Use a short sharp prayer of challenge.

The challenge of Jesus was to the point: "Come with me!"
Come with me!
And the powerless will band together.
Come with me!
And the despised will find a voice.
Come with me!
And the corrupt will be exposed.
Come with me!
And the bullies will be faced head on.
We hear the challenge.
We will take up this Jesus work.

The challenge of Jesus was to the point: "Come with me!"
Come with me!
And the rejected will find a friend.
Come with me!
And those searching for work will know patience.
Come with me!
And the chronically sick will be remembered.
Come with me!
And the downtrodden will take heart.
Come with me!
And the troubled one in our family, and friendship and church
   groups will be supported *(time of prayer and reflection)*.
Come with me!
And those who have lost loved ones will be embraced *(time of
   prayer and reflection)*.
We hear the challenge.
We will take up this Jesus work.

Follow the same pattern for the other sections.

---

2. Sing a verse of a hymn or song with "call" as a theme after
   each section of the prayer. For example, verse one of *Jesus
   Calls Us* (*Voices United* #562), or *Will You Come and Follow Me*
   (*Voices United* #567) or *Listen, God Is Calling* (*More Voices* #97).

4th Sunday after the Epiphany

LECTIONARY READINGS
Deuteronomy 18:15–20
Psalm 111
1 Corinthians 8:1–13
Mark 1:21–28

Jesus amazes people by the way he teaches.
Jesus has the authority to cast out evil spirits.

Give us, O God, a sense of your powerful authority in our world:
Then warriors will hold back from bombing first and thinking about civilians later;
Then politicians will put aside party interest in order to help the downtrodden;
Then the millions afflicted by AIDS in Africa and developing nations will get the drugs they need;
Then the poorest will be able to count on medical care and enough food;
Then developing alternatives to fossil fuels will be given priority and finance.
It is a different authority, your authority, O God.
It is care-full, it is visionary, and we see it in Jesus.

Give us, O God, a sense of your powerful authority among the suffering:
Then the challenged and elderly will be respected for all the gifts they have to offer;
Then the mentally sick will be taken as seriously as the physically sick;
Then those who provide healthcare services with compassion and empathy will be recognized;
Then patients will be able to speak openly of their fears.
We remember those who are ill at home or in hospital today (time of silent reflection).
Then the bereaved will know comfort, and rejoice that those we have loved and lost are safe within your loving care (time of silent reflection).

It is a different authority, your authority, O God.
It is care-full, it is visionary, and we see it in Jesus.

Give us, O God, a sense of your authority in the church:
Then those lay and ordered persons who are teachers and
   leaders will be nurtured in their ministries;
Then those who hang back from commitment will find and
   use their gifts;
Then those who encourage and help local self-help groups will
   be supported;
Then the wider work of the church will be recognized with
   enthusiasm, and given wholehearted support.
It is a different authority, your authority, O God.
It is care-full, it is visionary, and we see it in Jesus.

Give us, O God, a sense of your authority for ourselves:
Then we will take full measure of our abilities.
We will conquer our fears, and live with our guilt.
We will have the courage to follow our dreams.
We will find strength in working with others.
We will develop that essential spiritual part of ourselves.
It is a different authority, your authority, O God.
Your authority, O God, is personal, hopeful, and eternal.

Another Way

1. Before the prayer, talk to the congregation about the nature
    of authority: its universal significance, its use and abuse, and
    the times in our lives when we are in authority or are subject
    to another's authority. You might mention the way authority
    is experienced by young children and older adults. You could
    ask the congregation members to talk about specific positive
    authority persons in their lives, and those they would like
    remembered in prayer. You will probably hear of those who
    have used their power and influence in a negative way, and
    this will lead to prayer for victims of authority. You could use
    the four prayer sections as a framework for your questions
    and prayer.

NOTE

This approach to the pastoral prayer will be more manageable if you have one person talking about authority and asking the questions, and another composing and then offering the prayer.

We give thanks for those in our lives and experience, O God, who have been positive authority figures for us.
We thank you for good teachers who have provided knowledge, skills, and a fine personal example, like _____.

We thank you for local politicians who have served unselfishly and brought much needed services to our neighbourhood, like _____.
We thank you for the work of David Suzuki *(add any others)* who has alerted us to the challenges of global warming and the threat to wildlife survival as a result of urban development.
As we give thanks, Creator God, so we pray for those who experience harsh and abusive authority: those who are taken advantage of by their employer; the elderly in residential care; children who are bullied *(time of silent reflection)*.
For the exercise of good authority we give thanks, Loving God.
We pray for those who are ignored, abused, and victimized by persons in authority.

We give thanks for those in our lives and experience, O God, who have been positive authority figures for us.
We thank you for good ministers who preached faithfully and were pastorally caring, like _____.
We give thanks for church school teachers who taught with humour and sensitivity, like _____.
We give thanks for _____, who called on us to think of those who are supported by our mission fund offerings.
We give thanks for our moderator/bishop/national church leader _____ for carrying the responsibility of her/his position.
As we give thanks, Creator God, so we pray for those who are on the receiving end of harsh and abusive church authority:

newcomers to church who are ignored, aboriginal persons in residential schools who were ill-treated, youngsters who are seen as a nuisance *(time of silent reflection)*.

For the exercise of good authority we give thanks, Loving God.
We pray for those who are ignored, abused, and victimized by persons in authority.

2. Focus on the word amazing, and have in mind the amazing things Jesus did. This is a fully responsive prayer.

Amazing.
The powerful are humbled.
Amazing.
The very young and the very old are noticed.
Amazing.
The despised are seen in a new light.

Amazing.
Mental illness is seen to be as challenging as physical illness.
Amazing.
The sick are noticed and helped.
Amazing.
Hope received by those without hope.
Amazing.
The bereaved receive the support they need *(time of silent reflection)*.

Follow the same pattern for the other sections.

5th Sunday after the Epiphany

LECTIONARY READINGS
Isaiah 40:21–31
Psalm 147:1–11, 20c
1 Corinthians 9:16–23
Mark 1:29–39

Jesus goes away to a lonely place to pray but Simon and his disciples find him and say, "Everyone is looking for you."

Reflect the peace needs of your nation, neighbourhood, and social groups in this section of the prayer.
Our world citizens cry out for peace:
Peace in *(name countries and locations)* where conflict rages;
Peace where industrial strife is a fact of life *(name situations);*
Peace where politicians argue and rage;
Peace among racial groups;
Peace among family members who cannot get along;
Peace where there is struggle within sports/social groups.
**In the name of Jesus the peace-seeker, the peace-maker,
we pray for peace. We will work with those who are the
peace-bringers.**

The suffering hope for peace.
For those for whom a diagnosis has proved threatening, peace.
For those who are troubled by a lack of sleep, or *(problem with
a family or faith community member),* or a faulty gene, peace.
For those for whom an aging body has proved to be an
unhealthy body, peace.
For the young who are disturbed and puzzled by the effects of
illness, peace *(time of silent reflection).*
For those who have suffered grievous loss of any kind, peace.
For those who are dying, peace *(time of silent reflection).*
**In the name of Jesus the peace-seeker, the peace-maker,
we pray for peace. We will work with those who are the
peace-bringers.**

The church strives for peace.
Where there is loss, division, or disturbance in the local
faith community, peace. *(A known church situation may be
named.)*

Where the introduction of new ways to worship is a problem,
   peace.
Where local needs vie with mission projects, peace.
Where there is disagreement among members about a vision
   for the future, peace.
Where clergy and church leaders are hard pressed, peace.
In the name of Jesus the peace-seeker, the peace-maker,
**we pray for peace. We will work with those who are the
   peace-bringers.**

Individually, we look for peace.
In the turbulence of daily living, a peaceful time and place.
In the midst of a conflicted relationship or friendship, a way
   towards peace.
In the family unit, a consciousness of what makes for peace
   between differing members.
In the material word, a resurgence of the spiritual.
In the name of Jesus the peace-seeker, the peace-maker,
**we will be aware of our conflicts and unease and will
   give prayer time to search for and know your peace, O
   Most Loving God.**

Another Way

1. Use one of the hymns or songs with a "peace" theme after
   each section of the prayer. For example, *Come and Find the
   Quiet Centre* (*Voices United* #374), or *Make Me a Channel
   of Your Peace* (*Voices United* #684), or *Put Peace into Each
   Other's Hands* (*More Voices* #173), or *I Am Walking A Path
   of Peace* (*More Voices* #221), or *May the God of Peace* (*More
   Voices* #224).

2. Another prayer.

*The words and deeds of Jesus are "in demand" in our
   world today.*
There is uncertainty among those whose life has been upset
   by economic downturn. The uncertain seek stability in a
   trembling world.

There is fear caused by the threat of terrorist attack. The fearful seek peace in troubled times.

There is anxiety as a result of fast-changing technology. The anxious seek stability in a world where the pace of change is relentless.

There is insecurity among those who no longer trust the leaders, politicians, and powerbrokers. The insecure seek an order that is familiar and reliable.

Jesus speaks of peace, Jesus speaks of lasting values, Jesus speaks of healing, Jesus speaks of affirmation, and Jesus speaks of the need to question.

Jesus speaks and we will hear.

The words and deeds of Jesus are "in demand" among the suffering today.

There is uncertainty among those with unsatisfactory relationships. The uncertain seek to share deeply with family members and friends and receive reliable friendship in return.

There is fear resulting from undiagnosed medical conditions. The fearful seek peace through knowing what is wrong with them.

There is stress within homes, workplaces, and social groups. The anxious seek the calm that comes through troubles faced, and shared with a trusted one *(time of silent reflection)*.

There is an emptiness and numbness among those who have lost loved ones. The bereaved seek hope in the place where it seems there is none *(time of silent reflection)*.

Jesus speaks of peace, Jesus speaks of eternal values, Jesus speaks of healing, and Jesus speaks of the need to question.

Jesus speaks and we will hear.

The words and deeds of Jesus are "in demand" among church people today.

There is uncertainty among those who are searching for spiritual life. The uncertain seek ways that satisfy them, and a faith community that secures them.

There is fear because church attendance is declining. The fearful seek peace through understanding what is needed

to make the church a welcoming and mutually supportive
community of faith.

There is anxiety as a result of the difficulty in finding the
leaders necessary to make the church a joyful and serving
faith community. The anxious seek the calm that comes
through identifying persons with leadership skills and
giving them the necessary training *(time of silent reflection)*.

Jesus speaks of peace, Jesus speaks of eternal values,
  Jesus speaks of healing,
  and Jesus speaks of the need to question.
Jesus speaks and we will hear.

The words and deeds of Jesus are "in demand" by each one
  of us today.

We feel uncertainty as we look to what the future may hold.
We seek the ties of family and good friends to secure us, and
look for confidence to face what the fast-changing life scene
will bring.

We feel the fear that arises from goals not met and challenges
avoided. We seek peace through revisiting our goals and
facing up to people and events that cause us fear.

There is anxiety as a result of unreasonable demands on our
time and energy. We seek the courage to say "No!" and the
ability to carefully explain our reasons for doing so *(time of
silent reflection)*.

Jesus speaks of peace, Jesus speaks of eternal values,
  Jesus speaks of healing, and Jesus speaks of the need to
  question.
Jesus speaks and we will hear.

6th Sunday after the Epiphany

**(Proper 1. If this is the Sunday before Ash Wednesday,
this Proper may be replaced by the readings for
the Last Sunday after the Epiphany,
Transfiguration Sunday.)**

LECTIONARY READINGS
2 Kings 5:1–14
Psalm 30
1 Corinthians 9:24–27
Mark 1:40–45

*A man healed by Jesus makes a poor decision, and
there are consequences.*

We pray for the decision-makers of our world, O God:
For the sensitive and selfless politicians, and for the tyrannical
leaders;
For the careful and skilled teachers, and for those who simply
wish to impose their own way;
For those who work toward a sustainable life, and for those
whose concern is to take the most from the earth;
For the nurturers of the refugees and the poorest, and for
those who could care less about nurturing them.
**Enable us to support the faithful decision-makers, O God,
and expose the selfish ones.**
Followers of Jesus can do no less.

*We pray for the decision-makers among the suffering, O
God:*
For care-bringers to youngsters and elders, and for those who
disrespect the young and the elderly;.
For vocation-driven nurses and doctors, and for those
motivated only by profit;
For sick persons who know support, and for those who are
alone;
For social workers who keep strictly to the rules, and for those
who overflow with compassion;
We think of those in our own family and in our church family
who are sick and troubled.

We remember the bereaved *(time of silent reflection).*
Enable us to support the faithful decision-makers, O God,
and expose the selfish ones.
Followers of Jesus can do no less.

We pray for the decision-makers in the church, O God:
For crafters of new and exciting prayers and hymns, and for
those who keep slavishly to traditional forms;
For explorers of truth in scripture, and for those who see all
Bible writings as literally dictated by God.
For members who see neighbourhood mission as vital, and for
those who are reluctant to venture out.
For church leaders anxious to discover and use the talents
of all members, and for those who prefer to rely on the
same few.
Enable us to support the faithful decision-makers, O God,
and expose the selfish ones.
Followers of Jesus can do no less.

We pray for ourselves for the decisions we make:
For the times we are willing to hear fresh ideas, and for the
times our ears are closed.
For the times we engage in a new adventure in faith or
learning, and for the times we lack the confidence to change.
For the times we refuse a foolhardy course of action, and for
the times we lack the courage to say no.
For the times we support family members and friends at great
cost, and for the times we find some excuse not to.
We are followers of Jesus. Be with us when we are faced
with hard choices, O God.

Another Way

1. **Print or display the whole fully-responsive prayer.**

The healing path,
is walked by those who seek to protect refugees in *(current
situation).*
The healing path
is walked by peacemakers working in *(current situation).*

The healing path
is walked by those seeking to bring industrial conflict to an
   end *(current situation)*.
The healing path
is walked by those who strive to reduce the release of harmful
   gasses into earth's atmosphere.

 When we bring estranged family members or friends together,
we walk the healing path.
When we speak out for the downtrodden and despairing,
we walk the healing path.
When we are willing to leave past faults in the past,
we walk the healing path.
When we accept the help and assurance we sorely need,
we walk the healing path.

Follow the same pattern for the other sections.

2. Sing *Behold, Behold, I Make All Things New (More Voices* **#115)** after each section of the prayer. Or sing *Jesus' Hands Were Kind Hands (Voices United* **#570),** or another "healing" song or hymn.

7th Sunday after the Epiphany

(Proper 2. If this is the Sunday before Ash Wednesday, this Proper may be replaced by the readings for the Last Sunday after the Epiphany, Transfiguration Sunday.)

LECTIONARY READINGS
Isaiah 43:18–25
Psalm 41
2 Corinthians 1:18–22
Mark 2:1–12

Determined persons get what they want: Jesus heals their friend.

You call us to be determined followers of Jesus Christ – to have a vision of a new world, and to work to achieve it.
We have a vision of a world where there is no prejudice against racial characteristics or accent.
We have a vision of the world where the economically depressed are counselled and encouraged.
We have a vision of a world where artists and actors are respected and given the opportunities they need.
We have a vision of a world where those who struggle to learn find others to walk the learning path at their pace.
We have a vision of a world where peacemakers have the support they need.
We are determined to bring the vision to reality.
You, Loving God, go with us as a friend.

You call us to be determined followers of Jesus Christ – to have a compassionate vision for the suffering, and to work to achieve it.
We have a vision of adequate housing for all those who cannot afford to pay current rental rates.
We have a vision of training for those who are out of a job.
We have a vision of appropriate and timely care for those who are sick, especially for those who need surgery.
We have a vision of equal respect for the physically and the mentally ill.
We have a vision of support and friendship for all persons who have lost a loved one

(time of silent reflection).
We are determined to bring the vision to reality.
You, Loving God, go with us as a friend.

You call us to be determined followers of Jesus Christ –
to have a vision of a renewed church, and to work to
achieve it.
We have a vision of welcoming newcomers in a gentle,
personal, and inclusive way.
We have a vision of celebrating joy with members of the faith
community, and supporting them when hard times come.
We have a vision of being sensitive to the needs of the local
community and the wider church.
We have a vision of a faith community that does not exclude
those of other denominations or faith groups.
We are determined to bring the vision to reality.
You, Loving God, will go with us as a friend.

You call us to be determined followers of Jesus Christ – to
forge our own vision and to persistantly work to achieve
it.
A vision that calls us to use the full range of our talents and
skills, especially the ones we are reluctant to acknowledge.
A vision that reminds us that we can achieve much more in
collaboration with others than alone.
A vision that calls us to encourage and build up those who
doubt and struggle.
A vision that includes the spiritual as well as the practical
realm of activity.
Because you go with us as a friend, Loving God, we
believe our vision will become reality.

Another Way

1. Sing the first verse of *Be Thou My Vision* (*Voices United* #642)
   or the chorus of *Spirit, Open My Heart* (*More Voices* #79) after
   each section.

2. **Use the word determination as a response after each phrase of the prayer.**

Loving God, you number us among your determined people.
Determination
will enable us to name and expose prejudice.
Determination
will enable us to speak out for those struggling to make ends
   meet.
Determination
will enable us to support those who paint and act and write.
Determination
will find us speaking out and working for peace.
Loving God,
number us among your determined people.

Loving God, you number us among your determined people.
Determination
will enable us to make clear the place for prayer and praise in
   a world of spend, speed, and sport.
Determination
will enable us study the scripture with open and enquiring
   minds.
Determination
will take us outside of our comfortable faith community into
   the local community.
Determination
will free us to give generously to overseas mission work.
Loving God,
number us among your determined people.

Follow the same pattern for the other sections.

8th Sunday after the Epiphany

(Proper 3. If this is the Sunday before Ash Wednesday, this Proper may be replaced by the readings for the Last Sunday after the Epiphany, Transfiguration Sunday.)

LECTIONARY READINGS
Hosea 2:14–20
Psalm 103:1–13, 22
2 Corinthians 3:1–6
Mark 2:13–22

Jesus eats with outcasts. New wine in fresh wineskins. The new way of Jesus has begun.

Leader: New wine in new wineskins.
Congregation: **The old ways are finished. A fresh way opens up.**
Fast food is consumed without thought of nutritional or caloric value,
but one day the health value of food will be central and good nutrition the rule.
The supply of oil and gas is limited,
but one day the sun and wind and tides will provide our energy.
There are nations where children starve and many others are denied education,
but one day it will be the global right of each child to receive adequate food and education.
Many persons who want a job are denied one,
but one day work will be the right of every person and training will come without cost to the worker.
We will work for the new way.
It is the way of Jesus Christ.

New wine in new wineskins.
The old ways are finished. A fresh way opens up.
There are countries where basic health care is unknown or comes at heavy cost,

but one day medical care will be universal and free.
There are those who suffer pain and get no relief,
but one day pain relief will be accessible for all.
There are persons who suffer from cancers of unknown origin,
but one day the source of cancers will be discovered and treatment will be timely and effective. We think of friends, family members, and church family members who are sick at home or in hospital today *(time of silent reflection).*
There are bereaved persons who feel empty, lost, and alone,
but one day the bereaved will have the friendship and support they need. We think of those we know who are bereaved *(time of silent reflection).*
We will work for the new way.
It is the way of Jesus Christ.

New wine in new wineskins.
The old ways are finished. A fresh way opens up.
There are churches where the building represents the faith community,
but one day it will be the just and caring actions of members and friends that identify the church.
There are churches where the very young and the very old are seen as a nuisance,
but one day the wisdom of the elders will be sought after, and the profound questions of the young ones acknowledged.
There are churches where the focus of giving is to the local congregation,
but one day giving to the mission needs of the wider church will be as important.
We will work for the new way.
It is the way of Jesus Christ.

New wine in new wineskins.
The old ways are finished. A fresh way opens up for each one of us.
We hang back from declaring the unused skills and talents we possess,
but one day we will have the courage to acknowledge them and use them for the good of others.

*We have dreams for a future that is very different from
the present but cannot
find the strength to make change,*
but one day we will take heart and live our dreams to
discover the fulfillment of a new path.
We will work for the new way.
It is the way of Jesus Christ.

Another Way

1. Use questions to emphasize the theme.

Despised but holy.
Homeless persons searching for a warm place to sleep on a
cold night.
"In your face" beggars on the street corner.
Sex trade workers desperate for security in their work.
Older persons persistently looking for a job.
Who do we despise, God?
Who does Jesus see as holy?

Despised but holy.
Moms and dads being assertive in seeking learning help for
their children.
The chronically ill who insist on a second medical opinion.
Sick persons who say, "I have had enough treatment."
The dying who look for an assisted end to their lives.
Who do we despise, God?
Who does Jesus see as holy?

Follow the same pattern for the other sections.

2. Before each section sing *There Is Room for All* (*More Voices*
#62), or verse one of *There's a Wideness in God's Mercy*
(*Voices United* #271).

Last Sunday after the Epiphany
(Transfiguration Sunday)

LECTIONARY READINGS
2 Kings 2:1–12
Psalm 50:1–6
2 Corinthians 4:3–6
Mark 9:2–9

On the mountainside, Jesus is transformed before the disciples.

In your Spirit, O God, the world can be transformed.
Where there is the will for conflict, your Spirit works for
reconciliation and the peaceful way.
Where unemployment brings loss of confidence, your Spirit
brings hope and persistence.
Where young persons long to be understood, your Spirit
listens carefully and refuses to judge.
Where older persons are ignored, your Spirit remembers their
gifts and respects their wisdom.
In your Spirit, O God,
transformation will become a reality.

In your Spirit, O God, suffering can be transformed.
In the frustration of waiting for medical attention, your Spirit
pressures for more resources.
In the anguish of serious illness, your Spirit is the calming and
patient influence.
In the dark place of depression, your Spirit is the promise of
light.
In the void of loss and bereavement, your Spirit is the
comforting and supportive presence.
We remember those of our own family and our church family
who are going through hard times *(time of silent reflection).*
In your Spirit, O God,
transformation will become a reality.

In your Spirit, O God, the church will be transformed.
Where church members look only inward, your Spirit will

direct them to the needs of the local community.
Where there is a call for leaders and teachers, your Spirit will
speak to unused personal gifts and careful training.
Where persons long to know more about the Bible and
spiritual life, your Spirit will provide knowledgeable and
inspired leaders.
Where the church is set among strangers, your Spirit will
encourage the sharing of beliefs and sacred writings.
In your Spirit, O God,
transformation will become a reality.

In your Spirit, O God, each one of us will be transformed.
When we are challenged in so many ways, your Spirit brings
order, peace, and priority.
When we doubt our own ability, your Spirit brings self-
assurance and trust in our own gifts.
When we are afraid to venture out in new directions, your
Spirit tells us, "You can do it!"
When we fear the end of life and the reality beyond, your
Spirit reminds us of the love that will not let us go.
In your Spirit, O God,
transformation will become a reality.

Another Way

1. **Focus on being partners in radical change.**

Change beyond belief:
Into a world where economically strong nations give trusting
and graceful help to nations that are struggling;
Into a country where good agricultural land is preserved for
generations yet unborn;
Into a neighbourhood where the particular needs of the oldest
and the youngest are met with respect and generosity;
Into a society where those with different mental and physical
abilities find a good place to live and fulfilling work to do.
In radical change,
we are your partners, Loving God.

Change beyond belief:
Faith communities identified not by their building but their
  inspiring service of others.
Faith communities unafraid to search out the unmet spiritual
  needs of the neighbourhood.
Faith communities where music and worship resonate to a
  contemporary beat.
Faith communities that respect and value the scriptures and
  compassionate service of faith groups such as Buddhists and
  Muslims.
In radical change,
We are your partners, Loving God.

Follow the same pattern for the other sections.

---

2. Sing *Behold, Behold, I Make All Things New* (*More Voices*
   #115) or the refrain of *Spirit, Spirit of Gentleness* (*Voices
   United* #375) after each section.

---

3. Have a time of silent reflection after each section of the prayer.

SEASON OF LENT
Lent 1

LECTIONARY READINGS
Genesis 9:8–17
Psalm 25:1–10
1 Peter 3:18–22
Mark 1:9–15

Jesus is baptized and is tested directly afterwards.

Chosen, chosen by God.
Chosen!
Chosen to be a peacemaker, chosen to support the
  peacemakers *(name a local or national issue).*
Chosen!
Chosen to speak out against injustice *(name a local or national
  issue)* and to work for change.
Chosen!
Chosen to see the downtrodden and help them.
Chosen!
Chosen to take issue with the powerful and confront them.
Chosen, chosen by God.
We are among the chosen.

Chosen, chosen by God.
Chosen!
Chosen to stand with and encourage those who need a job or a
  voluntary position.
Chosen!
Chosen to notice and support the sick and depressed.
Chosen!
Chosen to be a voice for those too old or ill to speak for
  themselves.
Chosen!
Chosen to see those who have suffered loss and patiently go
  with them *(time of silent reflection).*
Chosen, chosen by God.
We are among the chosen.

Chosen, chosen by God.
Chosen!

Chosen to make clear the lasting place of the church in a fast-changing society.
Chosen!
Chosen to offer time and talent for the work of Christ's faith community.
Chosen!
Chosen to speak out for the work of the wider church in this nation and the countries where mission work is carried out.
Chosen!
Chosen to take the spiritual aspect of life seriously.
Chosen, chosen by God.
We are among the chosen.

 Chosen, chosen by God.
Chosen!
Even when the call seems to be to others.
Chosen!
In spite of our faults and shortcomings.
Chosen!
To leave the comfortable and predictable ways.
Chosen!
To find joy in the testing places, and peace when we should be afraid.
Chosen, chosen by God.
We are among the chosen.

Another Way

1. Focus on the theme of being tested.

 Jesus comes to the hard place of testing.
We remember those who are sorely tested in our world:
Those searching for a way to peace *(in the Middle East or current example);*
Nations with huge debts, nations without natural resources;
Able men and women who need access to educational opportunities;
Persons who lack food and need to access a food bank;
Children at risk of sexual or physical abuse.

At first the challenges seem overwhelming,
but when we start with prayer to you, O God,
hope grows and help is possible.

Jesus comes to the hard place of testing.
We remember those tested by sickness and loss:
Those lacking the courage to consult a doctor;
Persons in the first stages of dementia or other mental illness,
    and their loved ones;
Overworked medical and housekeeping staff members;
Those whose situations feel overwhelming;
Those for whom illness drags on and on;
All who feel a loss acutely *(time of silent reflection).*
At first the situation seems too much to handle,
but when we start with prayer to you, O God,
hope grows and help is possible.

Jesus comes to the hard place of testing.
We remember that the church is tested:
By the need for leadership and financial resources;
By the Sunday alternatives of leisure activities, sport, and
    shopping;
By the need to support missions and the wider faith
    community;
By the challenge of communicating the Gospel in a way that
    makes sense to non-churchgoing folks.
At first the challenge seems too great,
but when we start with prayer to you, O God,
hope grows and opportunities open up.

Jesus comes to the hard place of testing.
We remember that each one of us is tested:
When we feel the need to build up our self-confidence;
When we feel challenges in our friendships;
When we feel the stress of family conflict;
When we feel the weight of our years;
When we feel the call to new endeavours;
When we feel the challenge to develop our spirituality.
At first the pressure seems too great,
but when we start with prayer to you, O God,
hope grows and opportunities open up.

Jesus won through gloriously; that is the prospect you offer us.
We give thanks. Amen.

---

2. Sing a verse of the hymn *Jesus, Tempted in the Desert* (*Voices United* #115) after each section of the prayer, or do the same with the song *When We Are Tested* (*More Voices* #65).

Lent 2

LECTIONARY READINGS
Genesis 17:1–7, 15–16
Psalm 22:23–31
Romans 4:13–25
Mark 8:31–38 **or** Mark 9:2–9

Jesus tells of his forthcoming faithful journey to suffering and death. And – the Transfiguration.

We go forward in faith on this day:
Believing that the leaders of the world's powerful nations will find a way to avoid the horror of war;
Believing that the thousands upon thousands of threatened civilians will get the peaceful life they deserve;
Believing that those who seek terror and destruction will not take opportunities presented to them;
Believing that within our lifetime, no child will go to bed hungry;
Believing that refugees living in squalid camps will be resettled.
We go forward prayerfully,
for our prayers are the beginning of change.

We go forward in faith on this day:
Believing that the spoken and unspoken needs of the suffering will be heeded by their loved ones and caregivers;
Believing that those with power over the infirm and downtrodden will use that power wisely;
Believing that those facing hard decisions will find a friend to listen to them;
Believing that the bereaved will be able to express their guilt, anger, and emptiness to a loved one *(time of silent reflection).*
We go forward prayerfully,
for our prayers are the beginning of change.

We go forward in faith on this day:
Believing that our worship is the heart of our compassion and service in this faith community;
Believing that the church still has a crucial part to play in shaping our children and grandchildren;

Believing that there are fresh and Christ-like ways in which
  we can influence the local community;
Believing in the promotion of truth, justice, and service
  among members and friends here at *(name of church/faith
  community)*;
Believing that giving to the mission fund is as important as
  giving for local needs.
We go forward together,
we go forward prayerfully,
for our prayers are the beginning of change.

We go forward in faith on this day:
Believing that our Christian faith will hold us strong in the
  most testing times;
Believing that the Holy Spirit will give us the confidence to
  work in ways we had never thought possible;
Believing that joining our efforts with others will enhance our
  strengths;
Believing that setback and disappointment are the beginning
  of new opportunities;
Believing that our doubts are the stepping stones to a lively
  faith.
We go forward conscious of the disciples and ordinary saints
  who day by day lived the selfless life of Jesus.
We go forward unafraid, recognizing the simple, selfless
  example of Jesus Christ.
We go forward prayerfully,
for our prayers are the beginning of change.

Another Way

1. **Use the Transfiguration/transformation as the focus.**

In your Spirit, O God, the world is transformed.
Where there is the will to conflict and war, you are the Spirit
  working for reconciliation and peace.
Where unemployment brings loss of confidence and lack of
  self-esteem, you are the Spirit of renewal and determination.
Where young mothers struggle to balance a fulfilling career

and parental responsibilities, you are the Spirit that brings
new reserves of strength and patience.

Where those advanced in years feel their infirmity of body and
mind, you are the Spirit that encourages them to make the
most of the gifts and abilities that they possess.

Where the young grow impatient with the rate of change, you
are the Spirit that reminds them to take their time.

In your Spirit, Loving God,
transformation becomes reality.

In your Spirit, O God, suffering is transformed.

In the frustrating wait for medical attention, you are the Spirit
of active concern;

In the anguish and fear of serious illness, you are the Spirit of
calm;

In the dark place of depression and despair, you are the
promise of light;

In the void of personal loss and bereavement, you are the
abiding and comforting presence *(time of silent reflection).*

In your Spirit, Loving God,
transformation becomes reality.

In your Spirit, O God, the church is transformed.

Where the membership is older and slower, your Spirit
empathizes with the discouraged, yet looks for new
opportunities.

Where leadership is tried and tested, your Spirit encourages
the downhearted and thanks those who work unseen and
unappreciated.

Where the Bible is read but not understood, your Spirit brings
the best scholarship to light and calls for an openness to
fresh understandings.

In your Spirit, Loving God,
transformation becomes reality.

In your Spirit, O God, each of us is transformed.

When we are challenged in so many directions, yours is the
Spirit that brings order and peace.

When we doubt our own ability, yours is the Spirit that speaks
of confidence, assurance, and trust.

When our words and actions betray our faith, yours is the

Spirit that enables us to get back on the faithful path again.
When we struggle to find a new friendship or restore an old
one, yours is the Spirit that nerves us to make the first move.
In your Spirit, Loving God,
transformation becomes reality.

---

2. Focus on radical transformation in each section.

Radical transformation:
The agents of peace and reconciliation take centre stage in our
    conflict-ridden world.
Nations agree to carbon reductions.
Jail time acts to restore inmates to a productive life.
Politicians of differing persuasions listen to each other and act
    for the common good.
There are as many women business leaders as men.
Vision backed by action,
 brings radical transformation.

Radical transformation:
An end to a non-sustainable friendship.
A restoration of our sense of our self-worth.
A refusal to give in to apathy.
A willingness to forgive ourselves and others.
A willingness to acquire fresh skills.
A long overdue word of forgiveness spoken.
A long delayed word of thanksgiving delivered.
Insight backed by action,
 brings radical transformation.

Carry on in this format for the other sections.

Lent 3

LECTIONARY READINGS
Exodus 20:1–17
Psalm 19
1 Corinthians 1:18–25
John 2:13–22

Jesus goes to the Temple and drives out those who are buying and selling

There are people in our world that make us mad, Loving God!
People who get hooked on gambling and lose the family home;
People who use the Internet to take sexual advantage of
   young children;
People who take financial advantage of the unsuspecting and
   cause them to lose their life savings.
And there are some situations that make us mad!
The fact that some housing and industrial development takes
   place without regard to animal and plant habitats;
The fact that some children are denied basic health care and
   education;
The fact that some refugees are in camps for years before they
   are settled in safe countries.
These things make us mad, Loving God.
**Enable us to channel our anger into practical ways to
   bring change.**

**There are situations among the troubled that make us
   mad, Loving God!**
When people who are poor or mentally challenged are given
   the run-around by bureaucrats;
When employers are insensitive to family needs that have to
   be met during working hours;
When sports professionals and company executives receive
   huge salaries and pensions, yet service workers struggle to
   get by on minimum wage;
When sick people are not given the attention they need
   because they are old and without family;
When people we know well won't admit that they are sick or
   seek help *(time of silent reflection)*.

And we get mad when the bereaved are not treated with the
gentleness they deserve or given the grieving time they need.
These things make us mad, Loving God.
**Enable us to channel our anger into practical ways to
bring change.**

**There are people in the church that make us mad,
Loving God!**
Those who insist that the Bible is dictated directly to the
authors and editors of the scripture books;
Those who rigidly refuse to reconsider their religious beliefs
or express their doubts;
Those who see "the church" as a building and not as a
compassionate faith community;
Those who leave the leadership and congregational care to
others;
Those who give only to the local congregation and resist
supporting missions at home or abroad.
These things make us mad, Loving God.
**Enable us to channel our anger into practical ways to
bring change.**

**There are some things about ourselves that make us
mad!**
When we are called to respond to an unjust situation but
haven't the courage to put our thoughts into words;
When there are family or community situations that need
changing, but our apathy wins out over our will to act;
When the need to set priorities in life is clear, but we keep
putting off the hard decisions;
When our loved ones are crying out for help and we do not
know how to respond;
When our resolve to make a difference is overcome by fear of
the trouble this change in heart and action will bring to our
loved ones and us.
**Loving God, these things anger us. Enable us to channel
our hard feelings into a renewed willingness to
follow the example of Jesus, who spoke out and acted
promptly and with confidence. Amen.**

Another Way

1. Introduce the prayer as follows and focus on the issue of how the power of money can drive us to actions that cause harm.

The merchants at the temple at Jerusalem made large profits through the sale of sacrificial animals, and money-changing. Jesus considered these activities unscrupulous and a corruption of the religious centre and its worship task.

Money rules,
   and sports persons and business executives take home huge
      salaries and pensions while those on welfare and minimum
      wage struggle to get by.
It makes us mad!

Money rules,
   and sexual predators are able to advertise on the Internet
      without interference.
It makes us mad!

Money rules,
   and children in developing countries go to bed hungry;
      children in our country go to school without breakfast.
It makes us mad!

Money rules,
   and so-called financial planners take advantage of the
      unsophisticated, the infirm and the mentally challenged.
It makes us mad!

Money rules,
   and those who have the cash are able to obtain immediate
      medical treatment, while those lacking resources wait in
      line.
It makes us mad!

Money rules,
   and those challenged ones who lack a personal advocate

to help them obtain needed goods or services are quietly
ignored.
It makes us mad!

Money rules,
and those who are grieving are advised to quickly get over
their loss and resume their paid occupation.
It makes us mad!

Carry on in this format for the other sections.

---

2. Engage the congregation in a dialogue around the injustices
    that make them mad and incorporate the results of the
    conversation in a prayer. The best way to do this is to have
    one person dialogue with the congregation while another
    writes the prayer

Here are some questions to help you start the conversation:
What tragedies or disasters on the current international scene
make you angry? What can we do to help? If ideas are not
forthcoming, have some ready to share.

What recent local situations have made you want to write a
letter to the newspaper or call your city/town counsellor?
Give examples from a local newspaper or a local television
program. If you have written a letter or contacted a
counsellor recently, read the letter or refer to the discussion.

Thinking about those who are sick or suffering or depressed
or downtrodden, what situations make you mad? Give
examples from your personal experience or from a local
newspaper or television program. What situations compel
you to offer help or support? Ask persons to give personal
instances where direct discussion or confrontation has made
a difference.

What church situations make you feel angry? Some positive
examples that do not directly point to a congregational
situation or a congregational member might be useful here.

And – are there things about yourself that drive you crazy and
make you want to do things differently? Relate to people
differently? Act with greater courage? Give a personal
example of how an insight given by a friend or family
member has caused you to act differently.

Lent 4

LECTIONARY READINGS
Numbers 21:4–9
Psalm 107:1–3, 17–22
Ephesians 2:1–10
John 3:14–21

God loved the world so much.

We find that the needs of the world can be met in the Spirit of Love:
Love that exposes greed and exploitation;
Love that works out in the gym and follows a diet sheet;
Love that cares for children without limits;
Love that is aware of the needs of others in the
   neighbourhood.
We have seen that love in Jesus.
We will express love as we follow.

We believe that the needs of the suffering can be met in the Spirit of Love:
Love that accepts the need to move on;
Love that encourages the sick to seek help;
Love that patiently persists in the face of unresolved health
   problems;
Love that stays and comforts the bereaved *(time of silent
   reflection)*.
We have seen that love in Jesus.
We will express love as we follow.

We believe that the church can be a force for good in the Spirit of Love:
Love that welcomes the stranger;
Love that cares for the downhearted ones;
Love that brings hope to the despairing;
Love that includes all nations and creeds.
We have seen that love in Jesus.
We will express love as we follow.

We believe that each one of us can be renewed in the Spirit of Love:
Love that gives us the courage to begin again;
Love that enables us to face our weaknesses;
Love that does not give up on a friend or family member;
Love that is ready to risk and adventure;
Spirit-rooted love that reaches towards the Holy One.
We have seen that love in Jesus.
We will express love as we follow.

Another Way

1. **Use "love will win through" as the theme.**

Love will win through.
Refugees will be treated justly and resettled.
Those unemployed will find the support and retraining they
    need.
Those affected by events out of their control *(the weather,*
    natural disaster, fraud, corrupt officials) will find a listening
    ear and prompt practical assistance.
Love, even when tested, will win through.
Jesus patterns that love for us.

Love will win through.
The bullied ones will find someone to support them.
The depressed will find light in their darkness.
The sick ones will find strength and patience with family and
    friends around them.
The bereaved will find those to offer comfort and help them
    face their new situation.
Silently and out loud we remember those known by only us and
    those of our faith community.
Love, even when tested, will win through.
Jesus patterns that love for us.

Love will win through.
Church members and friends will feel loving friendship
    bringing them closer together.
God's love will encourage them to support the hungry,

the despairing, and the lonely through mission funds.
Love will deepen their creativity and strengthen their
   willingness to serve the needy in *(name of community)*.
Love will allow them to let go of the need to make a good
   impression, gain members, or appear superior to another
   faith community and to simply live in God's love.
Love, even when tested, will win through.
Jesus patterns that love for us.

 Love will win through for each one of us
and we will experience the love of close family showing us
   how much we are able to give and receive.
We will know the love of close friends who know us as we are,
   not as we wish others to see us.
Love will encourage us to do and be way beyond the limits we
   impose on ourselves,
Love will tune us in to the spiritual values that lie at the heart
   of this holy time.
Love, even when tested, will win through.
Jesus patterns that love for us.

2. Sing *Don't Be Afraid* (*More Voices* #90) after each section of
   the prayer.

Lent 5

LECTIONARY READINGS
Jeremiah 31:31–34
Psalm 51:1–12 **or** Psalm 119:9–16
Hebrews 5:5–10
John 12:20–33

Some Greeks come to Phillip and say, "Sir, we want to see Jesus."
The death of Jesus is close.

We want to see Jesus at work in our world,
proclaiming the Good News that men and women, gay and
   straight persons, and persons from all races have an equal
   part to play in establishing God's realm on this fragile and
   threatened planet.
We pray for *(name persons who have uncovered current
   situations of inequality)*.
We want to see Jesus at work in our world,
proclaiming the Good News that those who use their power to
   intimidate and threaten will be named and will no longer go
   unchallenged.
We think of *(name current situations of exploitation and
   intimidation)*.
We want to see Jesus at work in our world,
proclaiming the Good News that those who are at an
   economic disadvantage will be supported, respected, and
   offered retraining.
We pray for *(name those who are being offered help)*.
We see Jesus in those who walk the path Jesus walked,
and we give thanks.

We want to see Jesus at work among the suffering,
showing compassion to the forgotten and downtrodden,
   speaking out for those challenged mentally and physically,
   calling on the medical and social services to live up to their
   promises.
We pray for *(name situations currently calling for action)*.
We want to see Jesus at work among the suffering,
insisting that there will be housing in our area that is
   affordable and adequate, speaking out for the single-parent
   households, and those who get by on minimum wage.

We pray for *(name situations currently calling for action)*.
We want to see Jesus at work among the suffering,
standing beside those who are in pain, feeling their agony,
  making sure that they receive relief.
We think of those who are sick in our own family and in our
  church family, and remember our friends who are ill *(time of
  silent reflection)*.
We want to see Jesus at work among the suffering,
standing beside those who have lost loved ones, sharing time
  with those who are alone and afraid.
We pray for *(name situations currently calling for action)*.
**We see Jesus in those who walk the path Jesus walked,
and we give thanks.**

We want to see Jesus at work in the church,
ready to accept children as blessed beings who teach us and
  keep our feet on the ground.
We pray for those who teach and work with children and
  young adults *(name teachers and leaders)*.
Thanking those who care for and share leadership in the faith
  community, we pray for those who lead and pastorally care
  (name areas of church life where leadership is carried out).
We want to see Jesus at work in the church,
calling for the church to embrace a wider vision.
We pray for those who are concerned for the outreach work of
  the faith community *(name areas and people who are engaged
  in outreach and mission, locally and abroad)*.
**We see Jesus in those who walk the path Jesus walked,
and we give thanks**.

We want to see Jesus at work in each one of us,
challenging us to put behind us those times and events
  that have proved unworthy and care-less *(time of silent
  reflection)*;
readying us for the tasks that have our name on them, the
  faithful tasks that we have avoided *(time of silent reflection)*.
We want to see Jesus at work in each one of us,
calling us to the place of reconciliation and the encounter that
  will be painful for us *(time of silent reflection)*;
determined to make the most of the skills and talents we have
  kept hidden up till now *(time of silent reflection)*.

We hear the words and encounter the deeds of Jesus through good friends and family members. These valued persons inspire us to follow his pattern and example, **and we give thanks.**

Another Way

1. Focus the prayer on issues that crucify people.

The end of Lent. The end of the road for Jesus.
The self-serving powers, and the authorities he confronted, brought Jesus to the cross.
The ill-use of power and authority still exerts influence: whistleblowers are silenced, aboriginal persons face discrimination, workers are exposed to dangerous conditions, women are not given their rightful place, and qualified immigrants are denied work.
In solidarity,
we stand beside the crucified.

The end of Lent. The end of the road for Jesus.
The self-serving powers, and the authorities he confronted, brought Jesus to the cross.
Powerful authority figures still exert influence over the suffering ones:
Drug dealers dictate the lives of those with addictions;
Assertive friends want the shy ones to do what they say;
Some government officials go solely by the rulebook;
Some caregivers ignore the needs of elderly and infirm folk who have no family;
Some doctors treat the symptoms but are insensitive to the feelings of the patient;
Well-meaning family members tell the bereaved to, "Get over your loss." *(Time of silent reflection).*
In solidarity,
we stand beside the crucified.

The end of Lent. The end of the road for Jesus.
The self-serving powers, and the authorities he confronted, brought Jesus to the cross.

Authority figures still abuse their influence in the church:
We know leaders and teachers who insist on their own way;
We know faith communities where grass-roots opinions are
  not appreciated;
We know faith communities where those who lack confidence
  are exploited;
We know faith communities where those with a global vision
  are ignored.
In solidarity,
we stand beside the crucified.

 The end of Lent. The end of the road for Jesus.
The self-serving powers and the authorities he confronted
  brought Jesus to the cross.
Powers and authority figures still exert influence on us:
Sometimes we feel put down but do not speak up;
Sometimes we know we are oppressed, but do nothing
  about it;
Sometimes we know we are right but do not have the strength
  to go against the prevailing point of view;
Sometimes we feel mad at our oppressor but cannot find the
  right way to channel our anger.
We are among the crucified,
**and we will change our ways of dealing with
  oppression.**

Lent 6
Palm/Passion Sunday

LECTIONARY READINGS
FOR THE LITURGY OF THE PALMS

Mark 11:1–11 **or** John 12:12–16
Psalm 118:1–2, 19–29

LITURGY OF THE PASSION
Isaiah 50:4–9a
Psalm 31:9–16
Philippians 2:5–11
Mark 14:1—15:47 **or** Mark 15:1–39, (40–47)

Jesus comes to Jerusalem: triumph and tragedy.
The crucifixion of Jesus.

Triumph
Join the crowd and welcome Jesus with joy. Celebrate the
    victories:
When nations stand united with refugees and help them;
When transients and outcasts are noticed and supported;
When threatened minority groups have equal rights and feel
    secure.
Tragedy
Stand beneath the cross and feel the pain.
Experience the sorrow:
When people are casualties of warfare and political strife;
When qualified workers are denied jobs because of corruption
    or favouritism;
When rich agricultural land is covered with houses, and the
    lakes and seas are polluted.
In the triumph, in the tragedy, God went with Jesus.
As we celebrate with the joyful, as we stand with the
    troubled, God goes with us.

Triumph
Join the crowd and welcome Jesus with joy. Celebrate the
    victories:

The needs of the challenged are noticed and worked out;
There is shelter for street people in bad weather;
Those fearful for themselves and their relationships find
   insight and support.

Tragedy
Stand beneath the cross and feel the pain. Experience the
   sorrow:
Earth's richest nations are unwilling to share their resources
   with the poorest countries. Children go to bed hungry, and
   women are abused.
Obesity is an epidemic in North America and starvation a
   widespread reality in Ethiopia and Bangladesh.
Those chronically sick lack support, and the dying are left
   alone *(time of silent reflection)*.
In the triumph, in the tragedy, God went with Jesus.
**As we celebrate with the joyful, as we stand with the
   troubled, God goes with us.**

Triumph
Join the crowd and welcome Jesus with joy. Celebrate the
   victories:
The spiritual meaning of Christmas and Easter is taken to
   heart;
The giving nature of Christians is noticed and appreciated;
A willingness to question and doubt the biblical record is
   valued;
The place of Christianity as one faith among the family of
   faiths is hallowed.

Tragedy
Stand beneath the cross and feel the pain. Experience the
   sorrow:
Sunday becomes a day for shopping and sport, rather than one
   for worship and reflection;
Many persons have no faith to rely on, no faith to sustain
   them in times of trial;
The Word of God is ignored;
Leaders who speak out for the humanitarian rights of women
   and political prisoners are crucified.
In the triumph, in the tragedy, God went with Jesus.
**As we celebrate with the joyful, as we stand with the
   troubled, God goes with us.**

Triumph
We will join the crowd and welcome Jesus with joy. Celebrate
   the victories:
We follow our personal faith journey with enthusiasm;
We support and applaud those who persevere along the way of
   Jesus Christ;
We take our discipleship seriously and work it out with care.
Tragedy
Stand beneath the cross and feel the pain. In the shadow of
   the cross we are humbled:
We are aware of the superficial nature of our Christianity;
We realize how our actions seldom match our words of faith;
The need for us to gently speak of our faith to our family
   members and friends comes home to us *(time of silent
   reflection)*.
In the triumph, in the tragedy, God went with Jesus.
**In our faithful joy, in words and actions that would
   cause Christ to weep, God goes with us.**

Another Way

1. Engage the congregation with the question, "As you come
   to the beginning of Holy Week, what triumphs and tragedies
   come home to you as you consider our world, our local
   community, suffering, the church, and your own experience?"

2. A prayer based on the crucifixion.

Crucifixion. The wrong choice.
*Pilate answered, "Do you want me to release the King of
   the Jews for you?" They shouted back, "Crucify him!"*
There are demonstrations for lower taxes while the basic
   needs of those living below the poverty line go unmet.
There are demonstrations for more development in the mining
   and oil sectors, and the need to preserve the environment is
   obscured.
There are demonstrations for financial support to national

and local projects, but aid for developing countries is quietly
shelved *(time of silent reflection)*.
In the shadow of the cross,
our values become clear.

Crucifixion. Suffering without speaking out.
The chief priests along with the scribes were mocking him,
saying, "He saved others – he cannot save himself."
Authority figures are still insensitive. Their ears are deaf to
the needs of the vulnerable.
Authority figures are still insensitive. Older persons and
the very young who cannot speak out for themselves are
ignored.
Authority figures are still insensitive. There are line-ups in the
emergency wards and for elective surgery.
Authority figures are still insensitive. Those who have lost
loved ones are given immediate assistance but not supported
for the duration of grief *(time of silent reflection)*.
In the shadow of the cross,
our values become clear.

Crucifixion. Support when least expected.
Now when the centurion saw he breathed his last, he said,
"Truly this man was God's Son!" There were women
looking on...Mary Magdalene and Mary the mother of
James...
Faith community support comes from long-time church
members and friends.
Faith community support comes from those who yearn for a
spiritual life.
Faith community support comes from those who need a
community of welcoming and compassion.
Faith community support comes as local community service
projects are visioned and initiated *(time of silent reflection)*.
In the shadow of the cross,
our values become clear.

Crucifixion. A part of our own experience.
Jesus cried out, "My God, my God, why have you forsaken
me?"
We experience crucifixion when a long-time friend lets us
down.
We experience crucifixion when a family relationship is
shattered.
We experience crucifixion when a cherished work or leisure
project comes to nothing.
We experience crucifixion when a loved one is suffering or in
despair *(time of silent reflection)*.
In the shadow of the cross,
our values become clear.

3. Sing *Open Our Hearts* (*More Voices* #21) after each section of
the prayer.

Holy Thursday

LECTIONARY READINGS
Exodus 12:1–4, (5–10), 11–14
Psalm 116:1–2, 12–19
1 Corinthians 11:23–26
John 13:1–17, 31b–35

Jesus washes his disciples' feet.

We give thanks to God for those who serve.
Bowl and towel people.
You find them volunteering to serve meals to senior citizens.
Bowl and towel people.
You find them ready to speak out for the reduction of carbon
  emissions.
Bowl and towel people.
You find them offering to serve on the boards of local service
  groups.
Bowl and towel people.
You find them providing leadership in children's
  organizations.
Living God, we give thanks for those who,
like Jesus, fill the bowl and use the towel.

We give thanks to God for those who serve.
Bowl and towel people.
Where there is a need to stimulate persons who have suffered
  brain injury, they are there.
Bowl and towel people.
Where there is a need to assist sportsmen and women who are
  challenged mentally or physically, they are there.
Bowl and towel people.
Where there is a need to bring music and laughter to persons
  confined to an extended care facility, they are there.
Bowl and towel people.
Where the sick or pain-filled need a friend beside them, they
  are there.
Bowl and towel people.
When those who have lost loved ones need a listening
  presence, they are there.

Living God, we give thanks for those who,
like Jesus, fill the bowl and use the towel.

We give thanks to God for those who serve.
Bowl and towel people.
Church members and friends who Sunday by Sunday, year by
  year, give priority time and talent to their faith community.
Bowl and towel people.
Church members and friends who do the dishes and clean the
  sanctuary without looking for praise or thanks.
Bowl and towel people.
Church members and friends who give generously to the work
  of the local faith community and mission projects.
Bowl and towel people.
Church members and friends who encourage and thank the
  leaders and teachers of the faith community.
Living God, we give thanks for those who,
like Jesus, fill the bowl and use the towel.

Can we count ourselves in as bowl and towel people?
Are we on the look-out for opportunities to serve?
Do we do the jobs others avoid?
Are we willing to forgo personal pleasure and leisure time for
  the common good?
Are we ready to examine our bank of skills and talents and try
  out those we have not used before?
Living God, count us in as those who,
like Jesus, fill the bowl and use the towel.

Another Way

1. Weave the song *We Are Pilgrims* (*The Servant Song*) (*Voices
   United* #595) creatively into the prayer.

Good Friday

LECTIONARY READINGS
Isaiah 52:13—53:12
Psalm 22
Hebrews 10:16–25 **or** Hebrews 4:14–16, 5:7–9
John 18:1—19:42

The arrest, trial, and crucifixion of Jesus.

One: A forceful arrest.
We pray for those who are betrayed by their friends.
We pray for those who are forcefully arrested.
Two: We pray for those who are the victims of violent action,
and for those who use violence to obtain their own ends.
We pray for those whose just pursuit of a cause results in
persecution.
We pray for those who act first and think later.
We pray for *(name persons and situations)*.
We hold the victims in prayer before you, Just God *(time of
silent reflection)*.
One: *The cross-death of Jesus*
speaks to us and our time.
The cross-death of Jesus
calls us to prayer and action.

An unjust trial.
We pray for those who are victims of the legal system.
We pray for those who have no will to resist the powerful
ones.
We pray for those who are at risk in their own homes.
We pray for those in jails, hospitals, care institutions, and at
their place of work who are harmed and exploited by those
in control.
We pray for *(name persons and situations)*.
We hold the downtrodden in prayer before you, Just God.
The cross-death of Jesus
speaks to us and our time.
The cross-death of Jesus
calls us to prayer and action.

Cruelly crucified.
We pray for Christians at risk because of their faith: at
    risk of ridicule, at risk of being shunned, at risk of losing
    friendships, at risk of death.
We pray for church leaders whose work is ignored or
    criticized.
We pray for clergy abused by their parishioners, and for those
    who have been abused by clergy.
We pray for Christian aid groups that endure hardship in
    order to assist the suffering in situations of conflict and
    disaster.
We pray for *(name persons and situations).*
We hold the suffering faithful in prayer before you, Just God.
The cross-death of Jesus
speaks to us and our time.
The cross-death of Jesus
calls us to prayer and action.

Abandoned by friends.
We remember when a friend turned his/her back on us.
We remember when we could not forgive a friend.
We remember when we were ignored after a family quarrel.
We remember when we felt let down by a colleague at work.
We remember when we endured the hostility of group
    members at a leisure-time organization *(time of silent
    reflection).*
The cross-death of Jesus
speaks to us and our time.
Through forgiveness, reconciliation, and fresh starts,
we will turn abandonment into loving relationship.

Another Way

1. Sing *Jesus, We Are Here* (*More Voices* #189) or the first verse
   of *When I Survey the Wondrous Cross* (*Voices United* #149)
   after each section of the prayer.

2. Focus on present-day "crucifixions."

Jesus crucified then, crucified now.
Jesus hangs on the cross, betrayed, brutalized, victimized; his experience mirrored in those who are crucified today, for whom we pray.

Crucified in our world:

Refugees – ill treated, neglected and homeless because of political conflict *(name of country or area of world)*;

Older persons abused by those who should be caring for them;

Families forced from their homes by *(flood, earthquake, the economic downturn)*;

Workers without a job through no fault of their own, who feel shame and inadequacy.

Crucified by politics, crucified by those who have the power, crucified by natural disasters, crucified by a shortage of work *(time of silent reflection)*.

In the hard places of life,
we stand with the crucified.

Jesus crucified then, crucified now.
Jesus hangs on the cross, his experience mirrored by those who are crucified today, for whom we pray.

Crucified in our community:

Children with learning disabilities who are waiting for special help.

The working poor, whose wages are inadequate to support a family or provide decent accommodation;

Sick persons waiting for elective surgery;

Sick persons who are being treated for cancers.

Crucified by the loss of a loved one *(time of silent reflection)*.

Crucified by cuts to the budget for education, crucified by a lack of opportunity, crucified by a lack of money for health care, crucified by uncertainty.

In the hard places of life,
we stand with the crucified.

Jesus crucified then, crucified now.
Jesus hangs on the cross, his experience mirrored by those who are crucified today, for whom we pray.

Crucified in the faith community by:
Persons who see the building as more important than the
   women, men, boys, and girls who make up the church
   family.
*Leaders who will not listen carefully to the opinions and
   concerns of others.*
A lack of leaders and teachers.
Uncertainty over the meaning of mission.
People far away, whose names and faces we will never know,
   crying out for help from their Christian friends.
*Jesus, crucified by traditional views, crucified by poor
   communication, crucified by a narrow vision of "church"
   (time of silent reflection).*
In the hard places of life,
we stand with the crucified.

Jesus crucified then, crucified now.
Jesus hangs on the cross, his own experience mirrored by
   those who are crucified today. We pray for ourselves:
Crucified by our own apathy;
Crucified by the suffering or death of a family member;
Crucified by incidents in the past that we cannot let go;
Crucified by the sickness of a pet;
Crucified by poor mental or physical health;
Crucified by the effects of increasing age;
**Crucified by hopes and dreams that have failed to
   become reality.**
(Time of silent reflection.)
But Jesus did not stay on the cross, and neither will we.
A new day is coming for our world, for our community, for
   our church, and for ourselves.
The Friday darkness is upon us,
but the light will dawn. Amen.

SEASON OF EASTER
Easter Sunday

LECTIONARY READINGS
Acts 10:34–43 **or** Isaiah 25:6–9
Psalm 118:1–2, 14–24
1 Corinthians 15:1–11 **or** Acts 10:34–43
John 20:1–18 **or** Mark 16:1–8

The risen Jesus Christ.

 The tomb is empty, Jesus lives! *(Or after Easter Sunday:* **Death is defeated, Jesus lives!***)*
The world will be a better place!
The power of wind and sun and sea will replace the power sources that waste and pollute.
The abuse and exploitation of children will be unacceptable in every nation, and the wisdom of the elders will be heeded.
Peacemakers will find a way to end the conflict *(name current area of trouble).*
Weather experts will find ways of predicting floods and droughts *(current situation).*
Persons without jobs will find patience as they look for work, and those in unfulfilling occupations will train for a more rewarding occupation.
Artists will find an exhibition for their paintings, actors will get suitable parts, and musicians will receive the applause of an enthusiastic audience.
In the spirit of the risen Christ, the world will be a better place.
Jesus lives.
Hope is alive!

 The tomb is empty, Jesus lives!
The suffering will find relief.
The neglect and abuse of seniors living alone will be recognized, and stopped.
Those who have a prolonged stay in the hospital emergency area will experience sympathetic care and will be kept informed.
Mental sickness will be accepted as readily as physical illness.

Those who have lost a friend will find someone to listen to them.

Those who have lost a loved one will not be judged if they express anger or grieve openly.

We think of the sick and bereaved persons we know *(time of silent reflection)*.

In the spirit of the risen Christ, the suffering will find relief.

Jesus lives.
Hope is alive!

The tomb is empty, Jesus lives!
The church will be a faithful community.

Doubters will be given a voice and an opportunity to have their questions taken seriously.

Members will welcome newcomers joyfully and thoughtfully.

The Bible and other challenging books will be regularly studied.

The talents of each person will be sought out and used in faith community.

Giving for wider church needs will be seen to be as important as giving to the local congregation.

In the spirit of the risen Christ, a joyful church will praise and pray and share its enthusiasm.

Jesus lives.
Hope is alive!

The tomb is empty, Jesus lives!
Each of us will discover new life.

We will rejoice in new friends and companions.

We will contribute our best talents to the groups we belong to.

We will live with disappointment.

We will forgive the deepest hurt.

We will find ways to exercise our creativity.

We will overcome the threats to our self-confidence.

We will bring our dreams to reality.

We will find ways of saying the words that matter to those closest to us.

In the spirit of the risen Christ, nothing is impossible.

Jesus lives.
Hope is alive!

Another Way

1. **Focus the prayer on the theme of joyfully sharing the good news.**

The stone has been rolled away, the tomb is empty. Whom will we tell?
We will tell those who say, "The world can never be a peaceful planet."
We will tell those who believe that leaders will not listen to the downtrodden.
We will tell those who refuse to give the physically and mentally challenged a fair chance.
We will tell those whose shyness prevents them from making their presence felt.
Listen! Limitations are shattered and forgotten.
Death is defeated. Joy has broken out!

The stone has been rolled away, the tomb is empty. Whom will we tell?
We will tell those who feel they are too old or without the necessary training to get another job.
We will tell those who say, "Health care can never be provided fairly to everyone."
We will tell those who are in the grip of an illness that seems without end.
We will tell people in the dark cave of depression.
We will tell those who are in the tomb of bereavement *(time of silent reflection).*
Listen! Limitations are shattered and forgotten.
Death is defeated. Joy has broken out!

The stone has been rolled away, the tomb is empty. Whom will we tell?
We will tell those who believe that the Christian faith is outdated and irrelevant.
We will tell those who say, "This is not the time for change in the faith community."
We will tell those who have no time for prayer or spiritual practice.

We will tell those who see faith as a personal rather than a
community matter.
We will tell those who have no time for mission or outreach.
Listen! Limitations are shattered and forgotten.
Death is defeated. Joy has broken out!

 ***The stone has been rolled away. The tomb is empty. Whom
will we tell?***
We will listen to the wonderful news ourselves.
The news will remind us of times when we could have
given up.
The news will remind us of the need to give others a second
chance.
The news will remind us that we are not bound by mistakes of
long ago.
The news will remind us of our joy in friends and loved ones.
The news will remind us of all we are able to do to help the
despised and forgotten.
We will hear words spoken directly to us.
Listen! Limitations are shattered and forgotten.
Death is defeated. Joy has broken out!

2. Sing verse one of *Alleluia, Praise to God* (*More Voices* #59),
   or *Christ Is Risen from the Dead* (*Easter*) (*Voices United* #167)
   after each section.

2nd Sunday of Easter

LECTIONARY READINGS

Acts 4:32–35
Psalm 133
1 John 1:1—2:2
John 20:19–31

Jesus stands with the disciples and says, "Peace be with you."
Thomas expresses his doubts.

Peace be with you!
Peace for the peacemakers and peace among those who use
    violence.
We think of *(name current national or industrial situation).*
Peace be with you!
Peace for those who labour with the poverty stricken,
    and peace for those who struggle with job and home
    responsibilities.
Peace be with you!
Peace for those who work to bring quiet to the workplace and
    the environment.
Peace for those who choose the way of discord and raised
    voices.
In the presence of the risen Christ,
peace will break out.

Peace be with you!
Peace to physiotherapists who bring relief from pain,
and peace to those whose backs and limbs are sore.
Peace be with you!
Peace to dentists as they carry out their sensitive work,
and peace to those who suffer from aches of tooth and jaw.
Peace be with you!
Peace to medical professionals who bring healing and care,
and peace to those for whom pain is an ever-present reality.
Peace be with you!
Peace to those who counsel and reconcile,
and peace to those who have hurt close friends and family
    members.
Peace be with you!

Peace to those who stand with those who have suffered loss,
and peace to those for whom the death of a loved one is
   devastating.
Peace, deep peace, God's abiding peace *(time of silent
   reflection).*
**We believe that in the presence of the risen Christ,
peace will break out.**

Peace be with you!
Peace for church leaders who work hard to keep the faith
   community strong,
and peace to those who confront and disturb.
Peace be with you!
Peace to those who work actively to promote the justice and
   compassion of Christ within the local community,
and peace be with those who feel that community members
   should come to them.
Peace be with you!
Peace to those who search for spiritual truth through prayer,
   meditation, and Bible reading,
and peace to those who cannot work a quiet time into their
   day.
**We believe that in the presence of the risen Christ,
peace will break out.**

Peace be with you!
With me, Jesus? I often ignore my faith and give it low
   priority.
Yes, with you – no time like the present for a change.
Peace be with you!
With me, Jesus? My lifestyle leaves no time to take it easy.
*Yes, with you. I took time away to refresh and so should
   you.*
Peace be with you!
With me, Jesus? I have built up a store of grudges, obsessions,
   and hatreds over the years. I can't just let them go!
*I say, "Peace be with you, my peace, that the world cannot
   give." (Time of silent reflection.)*
**We believe that in the presence of the risen Christ,
peace will break out.**

Another Way

1. Focus the prayer on the theme of doubt.

Be honest, express your doubts.
"Unless I put my finger in the mark of the nails, and my
hand in his side, I will not believe."
I wonder if the abandoned children who live on the streets of
   so many cities will ever get the protection they deserve?
I wonder if the richest people will ever share their financial
   wealth with those who do not know where the next meal is
   coming from?
I wonder if the world's leaders will ever agree on a
   compassionate way to look after refugees?
Jesus said, "Do not doubt, but believe."
There will be a childhood charter to protect the most
   vulnerable on our planet.
There will be a way to enable the richest to share their
   resources with the poorest.
Refugees will find a permanent home where they will be safe,
   warm, and nourished.
Jesus said, "Do not doubt, but believe."
We believe!

Be honest, express your doubts.
"Unless I put my finger in the mark of the nails, and my
hand in his side, I will not believe."
I wonder if prisoners will ever know a system that seeks
   education and rehabilitation of those who languish in jails.
I wonder if the mentally challenged will ever find the
   community acceptance that they deserve.
I wonder if all those in pain will be able to control their own
   levels of medication.
I wonder if the dying will ever have the freedom to choose the
   time of their death *(time of silent reflection)*.
Jesus said, "Do not doubt, but believe."
There will be a movement that speaks not just of punishment
   but of rehabilitation.
There will be a way of funding sufficient group homes for the
   mentally challenged.

The movement to help patients to control their own pain and the time of their own death will grow.
Jesus said, "Do not doubt, but believe."
We believe!

Carry on in this format for the other sections.

---

2. At the end of each section, sing verse one of *Jesus Christ Is Risen Today* (*Voices United* #155) or *Hey Now! Singing Hallelujah!* (*More Voices* #121).

3rd Sunday of Easter

LECTIONARY READINGS
Acts 3:12–19
Psalm 4
1 John 3:1–7
Luke 24:36b–48

> *Jesus appears to his disciples and their mood gradually changes from fear to joy and wonder.*

The risen Christ brings joy and wonder.
Where the devastation of natural disasters is overcome
   through sharing, sacrifice and hope, the risen Christ is there.
Where the challenges of producing clean power are faced
   and the elements of water, wind and tidal currents are
   harnessed, the risen Christ is there.
Where education is tailored to the needs of students and their
   families, the risen Christ is there.
Where corruption is tackled head on and intimidation is
   exposed and countered, the risen Christ is there.
Where racial hatred is exposed and job discrimination
   outlawed, the risen Christ is there.
But it isn't easy. Luke writes,
**"They could still not believe,
they were so full of joy and wonder."** *

The risen Christ brings joy and wonder.
When the older infirm person accepts the need to move out of
   the cherished family home, the risen Christ is there.
Where a troubled person gets up courage to see her social
   worker or health professional, the risen Christ is there.
Where those persons who are addicted to alcohol or drugs find
   a person to stay with them, the risen Christ is there.
Where the youngster is able to expose the bully, the risen
   Christ is there.
When the whistleblower faces the wrath of her employer, the
   risen Christ is there.
When the person with cancer is free to ask the heartfelt
   questions, the risen Christ is there *(time of silent reflection)*.
But it isn't easy. Luke writes,

"They still could not believe,
they were so full of joy and wonder."

The risen Christ brings joy and wonder.
When our church comes alive with contemporary music and
   community programs, the risen Christ is there.
When our church reaches out to other local denominations
   and faith groups, the risen Christ is there.
When our church searches out and uses the talents of its
   members, the risen Christ is there.
When our church owns and supports the wider church of
   which it is a part, the risen Christ is there.
But it isn't easy. Luke writes,
"They still could not believe,
they were so full of joy and wonder."

The risen Christ brings joy and wonder.
When we are awestruck with the beauty of forest, mountain,
   or river, the risen Christ is there.
When we trust our best instincts and risk new ways of living,
   the risen Christ is there.
When we put unhealthy friendships behind us and make new
   friends, the risen Christ is there.
When we face up to the limitations of our work, our sports or
   social groups, and move on, the risen Christ is there.
When we acknowledge the spiritual side of our being and
   determine to grow spiritually, the risen Christ is there.
When we face the fact of our own mortality and make the
   most of each new day, the risen Christ is with us.
But it isn't easy. Luke writes,
"They still could not believe,
they were so full of joy and wonder."

* Good News Bible, Luke 24 verse 41

Another Way

1. Sing a verse of *We Meet You, O Christ* (*Voices United* #183)
   after each section.

2. Before the prayer, speak of the way the risen Christ can be found to be at work in situations of radical change. Have one leader dialogue with the congregation and another craft the prayer as the dialogue proceeds.

3. Focus the prayer on ways of seeing Christ risen in daily life.

Is Christ risen from the dead?
Look at those who strive tirelessly for peace *(names of negotiators/area of current conflict)* and know Christ is risen.
Consider those who work determinedly to ensure that at-risk children are safe and given the opportunities they need, and know Christ is risen.
Think carefully about those who struggle to care for persons released from jail, and know Christ is risen.
Be conscious of national leaders who have the interests of the most vulnerable at heart, and know that Christ is risen.
Reflect on the politicians who go against the power of big business to advocate for clean land, water, and air, and know Christ is risen.
Where the work of Christ continues, we can be sure Christ is risen, alive, and among us.

Is Christ risen from the dead?
Think about those who risk their lives to protect us: firefighters, police, and paramedics, and know Christ is risen.
Look at those who care compassionately for the physically sick, the mentally disturbed, and the deeply troubled, and know Christ is risen.
We pray for those dear to us and for church friends who are ill *(time of silent reflection)*.
Consider those who stand with persons who have recently lost loved ones, and others who feel that grief will never end, and know Christ is risen.
Think carefully about persons who seek to unburden themselves of guilt and fear, and those who strive to build up shattered self-confidence, and know Christ is risen,
Where the work of Christ continues, we can be sure Christ is risen, alive, and among us.

Is Christ risen from the dead?
Look at those who continually give time and energy to sustain
and build up the local church, and know Christ is risen.
Consider those who lift our eyes to the needs of communities
far from this town/city and know Christ is alive.
Think carefully about those bringing congregations and faith
groups together to proclaim the Good News in word and
deed, and know Christ is risen, alive, and among us.
Where the work of Christ continues, we can be sure
Christ is risen, alive, and among us.

Is Christ risen from the dead?
Bring to mind those who have been for you and with you in
the crisis moments of life, and know Christ is alive.
Reflect on those who have spoken the hard words that needed
to be said, and know Christ is alive.
Consider those who will not let you sell yourself short, and
know Christ is alive.
Think carefully about those who remind you of God's call to
serve faithfully and creatively just where you are, and know
Christ is alive.
Where the work of Christ continues, we can be sure
Christ is risen, alive, and among us.

---

4. Jesus tells the disciples, "You must wait in the city until the
power from above comes down upon you." (Luke 24:49)
Develop the theme of patience in a prayer and use the
response,

   "Give us, Loving God, the gift of patience."

4th Sunday of Easter

LECTIONARY READINGS
Acts 4:5–12
Psalm 23
1 John 3:16–24
John 10:11–18

Jesus the good shepherd.

Jesus the good shepherd
feels the horror of fleeing refugees who are in unknown
territory without resources. He stays with them and
protects them.
Jesus the good shepherd
will not desert the businessperson who is going through a
hard time, or the student struggling with a course.
Jesus the good shepherd
works sacrificially for the family member in trouble, and the
worker who is the victim of workplace abuse.
Jesus the good shepherd
brings people of diverse opinions and ways together for the
community good.
Are we ready and willing
to work as a good shepherd?

Jesus the good shepherd
goes out of his way to give special help to struggling school
children.
Jesus the good shepherd
insists that the elderly infirm and the very youngest patients
are treated with respect.
Jesus the good shepherd
refuses to take shortcuts when it comes to medical diagnosis
or treatment.
Jesus the good shepherd
encourages people to donate organs for transplant.
Jesus the good shepherd
is strength to the dying and comfort to the bereaved.
Jesus the good shepherd

prays for those are sick or tested today, and stays with them
(time of silent reflection).
Are we ready and willing,
to work as a good shepherd?

Jesus the good shepherd
cares for each person in the faith community.
Jesus the good shepherd
calls on church leaders to vision for the future, and to consult
fully with congregational members.
Jesus the good shepherd
asks those outside the faith community how the church can
serve them.
Jesus the good shepherd
questions the trusted and tried ways of worship and mission.
Jesus the good shepherd
has a world view when it comes to giving for mission.
Are we ready and willing
to work as a good shepherd?

Jesus the good shepherd
calls us to rejoice in our faith and talk to others about it.
Jesus the good shepherd
encourages us to stand beside the despised and miserable.
Jesus the good shepherd
reminds us of our ability to forgive and to start afresh.
Jesus the good shepherd
shows us how much can be achieved if we work together
with others.
Are we ready and willing
to work as a good shepherd?

Another Way

1. **Base the prayer on John 10:14, 15: I know my sheep and they
know me. And I am willing to die for them.**

God knows us and God loves us, beyond all limits.
God sees newcomers to this country receiving support and
God rejoices.

God sees refugees being turned away and God weeps.
God knows us and God loves us.
God sees the use of water, wind, and the tides to provide
power and God rejoices.
God sees rivers and seas polluted by mine tailings and oil
residues and God weeps.
God knows us and God loves us.
God sees sports helping youngsters and providing peaceful
competition in our world and God rejoices.
God sees violence tolerated in sports, and friendly
competitions turned into quests for financial gain and
God weeps.
Through sacrificial effort,
tears will change to smiles.

 God knows us and God loves us, beyond all limits.
God sees children and challenged persons sensitively
welcomed in church and God rejoices.
God sees barriers to the use of the sanctuary and buildings by
those who wheel and those who toddle, and God weeps.
God knows us and God loves us.
God sees careful questioning of scripture and teachings in the
faith community and God rejoices.
God sees a *take it or leave it* approach to belief statements and
the gospels and God weeps.
God knows us and God loves us.
God sees different faiths and denominations worshipping and
working together and God rejoices.
God sees violent acts and hatred spread in the name of the
Holy One and God despairs and weeps.
Through sacrificial effort,
tears will change to smiles.

Carry on in this format for the rest of the sections.

2. Sing the first verse of *The King of Love* (*Voices United* #273)
   (make the wording gender inclusive) or the first verse of *Love
   Divine, All Loves Excelling* (*Voices United* #333) after each
   section.

5th Sunday of Easter

LECTIONARY READINGS
Acts 8:26–40
Psalm 22:25–31
1 John 4:7–21
John 15:1–8

I am the vine and you are the branches…remain united to me.

Jesus, the true vine, will be known through the good fruit
   of the branches:
Peace and reconciliation *(current local or world situation);*
Hope in the midst of turmoil *(current local or world situation);*
Endurance where challenge or trouble are found *(current local or world situation);*
Encouragement at the start-up of a business venture;
Understanding where a business venture fails;
Friendship when loneliness is a reality.
Jesus is the true vine.
We will identify the branches, we will bear good fruit.

Jesus, the true vine, will be known through the good fruit
   of the branches:
Expressions of worth to those out of a job;
Encouragement to those who have been in accidents;
Dawning light in the darkness of depression;
Staying power when pain is a daily reality;
Patience when illness is long-term;
We pray for those we love and those we know who are sick
   (time of silent reflection);
Gentle advice when a person doesn't know where to turn;
Sustained listening when a loved one has died *(time of silent reflection).*
Jesus is the true vine.
We will identify the branches, we will bear good fruit.

Jesus, the true vine, will be known through the good fruit
   of the branches:
New forms of praise and prayerfulness in worship;
Giving that goes beyond generosity;

Solidarity with the weakest and most vulnerable, in and out
of church;
Practical concern that goes beyond the sanctuary walls,
beyond the neighbourhood,
and beyond national boundaries.
Jesus is the true vine.
We will identify the branches, we will bear good fruit.

 *Jesus, the true vine, will be known through the good fruit
of the branches:*
We will say we are sorry;
We will stand with the friendless;
We will link hands with others for good;
We will be done with apathy;
We will take up the just cause;
We will take time to smell the roses;
We will express our love and concern;
We will be faithfully confident.
Jesus is the true vine.
We are the branches, we will bear good fruit.

Another Way

1. Bring fertile soil, healthy vines in pots, a pitcher of water,
   branches, and grapes or other vine fruit into the sanctuary –
   they might be placed on the altar or Communion table – and
   offer the prayer below.

2. Dialogue with an accomplished gardener about the way to
   grow strong and healthy vines before offering the prayer
   below.

 Jesus the true vine.
The vine of Christ grown in good soil. (*Lift up a strong shoot
in a container of soil and display it to the congregation.*)
We pray for researchers and scientists who labour to develop
new strains of vines, fruits, and cereals.

We pray for teachers, tutors, and professors who impart fresh knowledge to young and inquisitive minds, and to older ones *(local schools, colleges, or universities could be mentioned by name)*.

We pray for tradespersons who instruct and guide the developing skills of apprentices.

We pray for parents and grandparents who provide security, the willingness to answer questions, and the boundaries within which boys and girls grow up.

If the vine is rooted in good soil, it will grow up strong and produce an abundant harvest.

The vine of Christ
for an abundant harvest.

Jesus the true vine.
The vine of Christ requires the right balance of moisture and sun for the branches to grow. *(Water a healthy plant.)*

We pray for those who foster a good climate in homes for the aged and clubs for young persons.

We pray for those who work towards a good climate in the workplace.

We pray for those who enable patients to freely express their symptoms and their fears.

We pray for those who gently take the hand of those who mourn and stay with them for the duration *(time of silent reflection)*.

If the vine has sunlight and the right amount of moisture, it will grow up strong and produce much good fruit.

The vine of Christ
for an abundant harvest.

Jesus the true vine.
The vine of Christ gives out healthy and productive branches *(Hold up a healthy plant.)*

We pray for those branches of the Christian church that make an impact within their community through vibrant worship, wise teaching, and modelling the just acts of Jesus Christ. And we pray for struggling faith communities.

We pray for leaders of the church who speak out for the Christian way and are not afraid of the consequences.

We pray for saints of the church who by deed and word

proclaim the relevance of Christ, at work, at home, and in
sports and social clubs.
We pray for those who are growing in the Christian faith
through questioning and expressing their doubts.
If the branches are firmly joined to the main stem of the vine
of Christ, they will produce good fruit.
The vine of Christ
for an abundant harvest.

 Jesus the true vine. The vine of Christ produces good fruit.
(Hold up a bunch of grapes, tomatoes, or other vine fruit.)
For strength to follow Jesus Christ and take his teachings to
heart, we pray.
For the ability to speak of our Christian faith to friend and
stranger, we pray.
For willingness to strive with others to work out of the spirit
of Jesus Christ in a world radically different from that of
first-century Palestine, we pray.
For the enthusiasm to support the Christian church in a time
of increasing indifference to its value system, we pray.
For courage to meet the challenges and setbacks of life with
the faithfulness of Jesus, we pray.
If the vine produces good fruit, others will see its value and
want to be joined to this strong stem as well.
The vine of Christ
for an abundant harvest.

6th Sunday of Easter

LECTIONARY READINGS
Acts 10:44–48
Psalm 98
1 John 5:1–6
John 15:9–17

*Jesus speaks to the disciples of his love for them,
a love that mirrors God's love.*

Give us your powerful love, O God.
In the midst of the world's troubles, your love is there:
Encouraging warring factions to seek reconciliation in
(present area of need);
Standing beside those who provide a safe place for the
homeless;
Advocating for drug companies to provide low-cost drugs in
countries without resources;
Exposing and confronting corrupt and powerful leaders;
Befriending the despised and those who are unable to find
regular work;
Working through non-governmental agencies like the Red
Cross and World Vision.
Drawing attention to the poorest and those at risk. We think
of *(give examples)*.
**We pledge ourselves to abide in your love, O God,
a love that brings change for good.**

Give us your powerful love, O God.
In the midst of those who suffer, your love is there:
Where men and women, boys and girls, are sick or face an
uphill struggle;
Beside those who have a life threatening illness;
Bringing reality to those who will not accept their lost
mobility;
Giving patience to those who are caregivers for persons with
dementia;
Sustaining those who are overwhelmed by anxiety or fear;
Comforting those who have suffered loss *(time of silent
reflection)*.

We pledge ourselves to abide in your love, O God,
a love that brings change for good.

Give us your powerful love, O God.
At the heart of your church, your love is there:
Befriending those who lead and teach in the local
  congregation;
Challenging persons who are apathetic and narrow-minded;
Singing through choirs and groups and happy congregations;
Giving vision to those who bring denominations and faith
  groups closer together;
Inspiring us to give for the needs of people in other
  communities and countries.
We pledge ourselves to abide in your love, O God,
a love that brings change for good.

Give us your powerful love, O God.
At the heart of each one of us, your love is there:
Bringing faith when we feel lonely;
Sustaining us in the tough places of life;
Challenging us when we are content with second best;
Encouraging us when we are reluctant to risk and adventure;
Encouraging us to share our troubles;
Reminding us to be gentle with ourselves;
Reaching out to those we love;
Bringing peace when we feel afraid.
We pledge ourselves to abide in your love, O God,
a love that brings change for good.

Another Way

1. **This Sunday is celebrated as Christian Family Sunday.**

**We give thanks for families, O God, and we pray for
  them.**
**We are part of the worldwide family, in a world of
  contrasts.**
A world where women are honoured, a world where women
  are abused.

A world where some children have every advantage, a world
where many children go hungry.
A world where some challenged ones are seen as an example,
a world where some challenged ones are seen as a problem.
A world where the wisdom of the elderly is celebrated, a
world where the elderly infirm are hidden away.
A world where gifts and skills are fostered, a world where
talent is ignored.
A world where the homeless are forgotten, a world where
street people are supported.
As we pray for mothers, children, the elderly, and those
without a home,
Loving God,
inspire us to bring the changes Jesus would want.

**We give thanks for families, O God, and we pray for
them.**
We belong to human families, families of contrasts.
Families where mothers are finding fulfillment through
bringing up their children, and families where mothers are
frustrated because they have no time for work that satisfies
them.
Families brimming over with energy and good humour, and
families tested by job loss and debt.
Families where sports and exercise are routine, and families
where there is no interest in play or keeping fit.
Families where the members are healthy, and families
struggling with ill health.
Families rejoicing at a new birth, and families where
bereavement has created an aching void *(time of reflection).*
As we pray for mothers, tested families, families where there
is illness, and those who have lost loved ones,
Loving God,
inspire us to bring the changes Jesus would want.

We give thanks for families, O God, and we pray for them.
**We are members of the church family, a family of
contrasts.**
We pray for *(name of our church),* and other faith communities
of our denomination in this nation and throughout the
world;

Thriving churches where membership is growing and
enthusiasm is infectious, and churches just trying to stay
alive;
Churches that focus on practical help to the downcast and
challenged, churches that focus on singing and drama,
churches that focus on family programs and teaching.
Churches where giving to those outside their walls is second
nature, churches where all efforts are directed to their own
needs.
As we pray for the leaders and teachers at *(name of local
church)*,
As we pray for those faith communities that are going through
testing times,
As we pray that churches appreciate and give money for the
needs of faith communities beyond our shores *(time of
reflection)*,
Loving God,
inspire us to bring the changes Jesus would want.

 **We give thanks for families, O God, and we pray for
them.**
**You have put each one of us in a family, O God, a family
of contrasts.**
There are family members who support and help us, and there
are those who hinder us and bruise our self-esteem;
There are family members who have special challenges at this
time, and those for whom this is a time of celebration;
There are family members with whom we are able to share
and those who keep us at arm's-length;
There are family members who find joy in their faith, and
those who are indifferent to the Way of Jesus Christ.
And there are needs that we can only share with you, Our
God *(time of reflection)*.
As we pray for the family which is ours, in its great moments
and its sorrows, its deepest need,
Loving God,
inspire us to bring the changes Jesus would want.

---

2. Sing *You Are My Father* (*More Voices* #105), *Who Is My Mother*
   (*More Voices* #178) or verse one of *Would You Bless Our Homes
   and Families* (*Voices United* #556) after each section.

3. A prayer for mothers on Christian Family Sunday.

Loving and Eternally Caring God, we give you thanks for those who are mothers. Our prayers are for them.
We pray for parents and children who have been hurt in domestic accidents, and we remember those who advocate for home safety.
We pray for those who enjoy the call of parenting and home-making.
We think of mothers who balance a fulfilling job with caring for the children they love.
We pray for those who are caught in the bind of working long hours for minimum wage and caring for the children they love.
We pray for grandparents as they care for their grandchildren; for the joy and the responsibility that this care entails.
In moments of silence, we bring before you the names of those who we know, and offer to you, O God, their joys and needs *(time of silent reflection)*.
Mother God,
inspire us to help and support those for whom we have prayed.

Loving and Eternally Caring God, we pray for mothers, and others, who are hard-tested by abuse, sickness, and stress.
We pray for mothers in *(name of country)* who have to deal with famine, homelessness, or abuse.
We pray for mothers in *(name of country)* where domestic violence is an everyday fact of life, and we remember the work of our local shelter *(name)* for mothers fleeing violence.
We remember those who would like to experience motherhood but are unable to do so.
We pray for women who are pregnant unexpectedly, in the decisions they have to take.
We pray for mothers who, though ill, keep the home going and the family together.
We bring before you, O God, our own family members, and church family members who are sick or troubled today.
We pray for families who have lost loved ones, and we

remember parents and children who have died *(time of silent reflection)*.

Most Loving God, you are with family members, especially mothers, who are tried and frustrated at this time. We recognize that these were just the sort of persons Jesus stood with, encouraged, and cared for.

Enliven this faith community in its efforts to stand with those who are mothers.

Mother God,
inspire us to help and support those for whom we have prayed.

4. Have family members of different generations offer separate sections of the prayers.

5. Have one worship leader dialogue with the congregation about what makes a good world, church, and human family, while another crafts a prayer to offer.

7th Sunday of Easter

LECTIONARY READINGS
Acts 1:15–17, 21–26
Psalm 1
1 John 5:9–13
John 17:6–19

Jesus prays for those who are his committed followers.

Committed to Jesus Christ, we know where we stand in this world.
We stand for the rights of all the world's children to food,
shelter, and a basic education.
We stand with refugees in their quest for food and drink, a
new homeland, and protection from violence.
We stand with women who are abused and dominated.
We stand with those who are tortured and imprisoned without
cause.
We stand for an end to warfare as a way of settling disputes,
and for friendship and sport as the way of working out the
rivalries of nations.
We stand with the differently gifted that they may lead happy
and fulfilling lives.
We stand against dictatorship and for those leaders who listen
to the joys and needs of ordinary people.
Jesus knew where he stood.
We will advance his values in our day and generation.

Committed to Jesus Christ, we stand with those who suffer.
We stand with those who cannot read a road sign or a
newspaper in their quest for literacy.
We stand with those who believe that drugs and medical and
dental treatment should be provided for all who need them.
We stand with children who, for lack of encouragement and a
quiet space, cannot get their homework completed.
We stand with those who provide music, exercise, and games
for nursing home patients.
We stand with those who cannot rid themselves of pain.
We stand with those who are worried by an ache or pain but
are unwilling to see the doctor.

We stand with those who are caught up in a web of
bereavement or loss *(time of silent reflection)*.
Jesus was compassionately concerned for the sick and helped
them.
Jesus knew where he stood.
We will advance his values in our day and generation.

Committed to Jesus Christ, we stand with faith community
members.
We stand with those who believe in the relevancy of the
present-day church.
We stand with those who sing and dance and make lilting
music to praise their God.
We stand with those who provide spiritual leadership to the
local faith community *(names of clergy and other spiritual*
leaders).
We stand with those in the wider church who support and
help us here *(names and areas of leadership in the wider*
church).
We stand with those who challenge us to serve the most
pressing needs of the local community.
We stand with those who advocate for political prisoners and
others who are in jail.
We stand with those who challenge us to give beyond our
means to those beyond our national boundaries.
Jesus supported the faith community of his time but was not
afraid to make clear the errors of its leaders.
Jesus knew where he stood.
We will advance his values in our day and generation.

Committed to Jesus Christ, we know God stands with us.
God sees our tendency to apathy and taking the easy way, and
calls us to action and rigour.
God stays with us when the testing time comes and refuses to
give up on us, even when we give up on ourselves.
God calls us to rejoice in our family and faith communities
and to work with others to build up both.
God laughs with us when we share a good joke and cries with
us when we let a best friend down.
God calls us to health of body and mind, and is with us as we
work out in the gym or read an insightful book.

For Jesus, the presence of God was a moment by moment
reality.
God gave him a purpose and a faithful direction.
Jesus knew where he stood.
We will advance his values in our day and generation.

Another Way

1. Sing a commitment to Christ after each section of the prayer.
   Sing a verse of *Take My Life and Let It Be* (*Voices United* #506)
   or *Three Things I Promise* (*More Voices* #176) or *Who Is My
   Mother* (*More Voices* #178) (Holy Communion).

ASCENSION OF THE LORD

LECTIONARY READINGS
Acts 1:1–11
Psalm 47 **or** Psalm 93
Ephesians 1:15–23
Luke 24:44–53

Jesus is ascended; the disciples wait for the coming of the Holy Spirit at Pentecost.

Waiting isn't easy.
The world's poorest still don't know where the next meal is coming from.
Waiting isn't easy.
Demands for a reduction of greenhouse gas emissions are still ignored in the name of big company profit.
Waiting isn't easy.
Prisoners are still not offered the life-skills and job training that will keep them from reoffending.
Waiting isn't easy.
Young children are still abused by their parents and foster parents.
Waiting isn't easy.
The seas are still polluted by the garbage of developed nations.
The disciples waited in hope for the Holy Spirit,
and we will work joyfully for our hope to become
reality.

Waiting isn't easy.
Young persons looking for their first job still feel discouraged.
Waiting isn't easy.
Some drugs and diagnostic services are still in short supply.
Waiting isn't easy.
Those with depression and mental illness are still overlooked and marginalized.
Waiting isn't easy.
Chronically sick persons still lack constant friends.
Waiting isn't easy.
The bereaved are still told to put their grieving behind them.
We pray for those waiting for opportunity, those waiting for

recognition, those waiting for healing, those waiting for
their aching sense of loss to subside *(time of silent reflection)*.
The disciples waited in hope for the Holy Spirit,
**and we will work joyfully for our hope to become
reality.**

Waiting isn't easy.
Church members still believe that Sunday worship will once
again take priority over sports and shopping on the "day of
rest."
Waiting isn't easy.
Church leaders still long for the time when there will
be a steady stream of younger persons ready to take on
their jobs.
Waiting isn't easy.
Those who wheel and those who lack mobility still look for
the time when their needs are fully met within the faith
community.
Waiting isn't easy.
Communities supported by mission funds still dream of the
time when their pressing needs stir us to a generosity that
hurts.
The disciples waited in hope for the Holy Spirit,
**and we will work joyfully for our hope to become
reality.**

Waiting isn't easy.
We wait for a new friend to come along but there is no one
in sight.
Waiting isn't easy.
We wait for the justified apology to be offered, but we wait
in vain.
Waiting isn't easy.
We wait for a family quarrel to end, but it drags on and on.
Waiting isn't easy.
We wait for deserved recognition for a job well done, but
another gets the praise.
Waiting isn't easy.
We wait for spiritual revelation, but there is no mystical voice.
The disciples waited in hope for the Holy Spirit,
**and we will work joyfully for our hope to become
reality.**

PENTECOST SUNDAY

LECTIONARY READINGS
Acts 2:1–21 **or** Ezekiel 37:1–14
Psalm 104:24–34, 35b
Romans 8:22–27 **or** Acts 2:1–21
John 15:26–27, 16:4b–15

The coming of the Holy Spirit.

Your Spirit is on fire for us, working with us, Loving God:
Bringing hope for peace to the troubled people of the Middle East *(or current situation);*
Bringing hope for an end to stress and suffering for those affected by industrial unrest/conflict *(current situation);*
Bringing hope for normal life again *(to those affected by a natural disaster);*
Bringing hope for work to those unable to find a job;
Bringing hope for news about *(local missing person's story).*
Your Spirit is alive for us.
Bless us as we work with your Holy Spirit.

Your Spirit is on fire for us, working with us, Loving God:
A source of community to those who feel they are on their own;
A source of inspiration to those who feel like a failure;
A source of healing to those who are troubled in their minds;
A source of renewal to those who despair of being healed in their bodies;
A source of joy to those who know an end to suffering;
A source of peace to the dying;
A source of warm companionship to those who are in the cold place of bereavement *(time of silent reflection).*
Your Spirit is alive for us.
Bless us as we work with your Holy Spirit.

Your Spirit is on fire for us, working with us, Loving God:
Bringing mutual support to this local community of faith;
Inspiring the clergy/ministers/pastors;
Encouraging the leaders and board/session members;

Showing patience and creativity with adult/junior church
teachers and youth group leaders;
Giving insight to those who work for *(the national
denomination magazine)* as they challenge the national
church and report on community and mission work
overseas.
And your Spirit is with the overseas actions for good of
(denomination), which we support through our mission
fund.
Your Spirit is alive for us.
Bless us as we work with your Holy Spirit.

*And your Spirit is on fire and working within each one
of us:*
Reminding us of the Christian heritage in which we grow and
mature;
Strengthening us to endure in the testing experiences of life;
Giving us flexibility and patience as we try new endeavours;
Opening us to fresh ways of looking at the world and those
we love;
Calling us to rejoice in our faith, and to proclaim it in word
and action.
To your Holy Spirit, O God, there before we were born,
present with us today, and with us through eternity,
we offer these prayers in the name of Jesus Christ,
**in whom your Spirit lived and moved and had abundant
life.**

Another Way

1. **Use a fully responsive prayer format focusing on movement of
Spirit.**

Moved by the Spirit
the terror-bringers will be exposed.
Moved by the Spirit
the peacemakers will win through. We pray for *(international
situation)*.
Moved by the Spirit
every child will know security and love. We pray for *(local
child neglect situation)*.

Moved by the Spirit
industrial peace will be the reality.
Moved by the Spirit
rich nations will share with poor. We pray for *(nation in need of support)*.
The Spirit moves,
and hope returns.

 Moved by the Spirit
those troubled by debt will find a counsellor.
Moved by the Spirit
those who have lost the resolve to look for a job will be encouraged.
Moved by the Spirit
those who are addicted will accept that they need help. We pray for members of Alcoholics Anonymous, Narcotics Anonymous…
Moved by the Spirit
those who have not faced their sickness will reveal its presence to another person.
Moved by the Spirit
those who have lost a loved one will openly express their grief *(time of silent reflection)*.
The Spirit moves,
and hope returns.

Follow the same pattern for the other sections.

2. Sing a "spirit" song or hymn after each section. Some suggestions: *Veni Sancte Spiritus (More Voices #75)*; the chorus of *Spirit, Open My Heart (More Voices #79)*; the first verse of *There's a Spirit in the Air (Voices United #582)*.

3. Focus the prayer on the valley of the dry bones (Ezekiel 37:1–14).

To start each section of the prayer, either sing *Dem bones, dem bones, dem dry bones,*
Now hear the word of the Lord twice, or say, *"These are dry bones."*

These are dry bones:
Managers who turn a blind eye to fast-moving changes in data
   processing;
Parents who refuse to give their children clear boundaries;
Politicians who refuse to listen to the grass-roots voice;
Sportspersons who rely on drugs to achieve results;
Electricity providers who refuse to consider the sun, the wind,
   or the ocean as potential sources of energy.
The dry bones need the Spirit.
Then they will come alive.

These are dry bones:
Worship leaders who refuse to try out new ways of praying
   to God;
Musicians who are content with the traditional hymns;
Church members who give only to the local faith community;
Faith groups that refuse to reach out to other faith groups in
   the neighbourhood;
Church groups that do not consider the needs of the local
   community.
The dry bones need the Spirit.
Then they will come alive.

Follow the same pattern for the other sections, then all sing:

The toe bone connected to the heel bone,
The heel bone connected to the foot bone,
The foot bone connected to the leg bone,
The leg bone connected to the knee bone,
The knee bone connected to the thigh bone,
The thigh bone connected to the back bone,
The back bone connected to the neck bone,
The neck bone connected to the head bone,
Oh, hear the word of the Lord!

Dem bones, dem bones, gonna walk aroun'
Dem bones, dem bones, gonna walk aroun'
Dem bones, dem bones, gonna walk aroun'
Oh, hear the word of the Lord.

SEASON AFTER PENTECOST
Trinity Sunday
1st Sunday after Pentecost

LECTIONARY READINGS
Isaiah 6:1–8
Psalm 29
Romans 8:12–17
John 3:1–17

No one can see the Kingdom of God without being born again.

Is it time for the leaders of our world to be born again?
(Reflect on contemporary needs in this section of the prayer.)
To see the poorest ones as sisters and brothers and offer them help.
To make sure that refugees do not wait endlessly in camps before being resettled.
To recognize that a full-time job brings not just a wage, but self-confidence.
To work freely with other countries to reduce the amount of carbon gases released into the atmosphere.
To take to heart the needs of those with mental and physical challenges, and meet those needs.
The time has come for rebirth.
We are followers of Jesus Christ. We encourage changes in attitude and positive actions.

Is it time for those who work with the suffering to be born again?
To ensure that those with addictions or in financial crisis get the help they need.
To speak out against the traumatic treatment of chickens, cattle, and fish raised for food.
To refuse to allow a lack of money to be a barrier to diagnosis or treatment of illness.
To make clear that neglect and abuse of the elderly infirm is unacceptable.
To advocate for those who face a long wait before diagnosis.
To give those who have lost loved ones time to come to terms with their loss *(time of silent reflection).*
The time has come for rebirth.

We are followers of Jesus Christ. We encourage changes in attitude and positive actions.

Is it time for those who work in the church to be born again?
To welcome those who do not fit "polite society" into the church.
To focus the church more on the needs of the neighbourhood and less on the needs of its own members.
To recognize the power that comes from small groups eating and studying together.
To thank wholeheartedly those who are well-known as church leaders and those who work quietly in the background *(time of silent reflection).*
The time has come for rebirth.
We are followers of Jesus Christ. We encourage changes in attitude and positive action.

Is it time for each one of us to be born again?
To rejoice in God's blessings and voice our thanks in prayer and praise.
To recognize our shortcomings and take the first steps to change our ways.
To think carefully about our values and align them in the light of Christ.
To reflect on family members who we take for granted and give them a gift.
To cease from struggle and know the Peace of God.
We *will be* reborn, and our attitudes and actions will make this clear.

Another Way

1. Focus the prayer on "God loved the world so much that God gave Jesus to the world."

A Prayer for Trinity Sunday

Love beyond imagining.
The Love of God:
The source of creation and the driving force for all those who
seek to keep creation good. We pray for *(current action to
work for clean air or clean water)*.
The author of justice and supporter of those who work for a
just and compassionate world. We pray for *(current action to
fight oppression, gender bias, or corruption)*.
Peace-bringer for all the ages, and inspiration to those who
seek an end to war. We pray for *(current action to bring peace
to an area of conflict)*.
***Beyond all imagining, beyond all limits, beyond all time,
endless, engaging, ever-present Love.***

Love beyond imagining.
The Love of Jesus Christ:
Invites new beginnings as followers. We pray for *(current local
or overseas area where new beginnings are happening)*.
Befriends the suffering, wherever they might be found. We
pray for *(current local or overseas area wherever people are sick
or suffering)*.
Recognizes and supports the mentally sick. We pray for
*(current local or overseas area where those who are mentally
challenged are suffering)*.
Stands beside those who mourn. We pray for those in our
family, and in our friendship and church circles who have
suffered loss *(time of silent reflection)*.
***Beyond all imagining, beyond all limits, beyond all time,
endless, engaging, ever-present Love.***

Love beyond imagining.
The Holy Spirit at work with Love:
Encourages struggling faith communities. We pray for *(current
areas of struggle in the local or overseas church)*.
Encourages those with different talents and skills to work
together for Jesus Christ. We pray for *(current area of
ecumenical or interfaith action)*.
Inspires those who look for a spiritual life. We pray for those
who are searching for a dimension of life that is not satisfied
by sport, occupation, or social pursuits.

Beyond all imagining, beyond all limits, beyond all time,
endless, engaging, ever-present Love.

All-embracing love,
Love beyond imagining,
Love beyond expression,
Love for each one of us.
Celebrating with us in times of joy.
Challenging us to venture and risk, refusing to be satisfied
    with the way things are.
Countering our fear with courage.
Enabling us to cooperate with others.
Showing us the path of justice and compassion.
Beyond all imagining, beyond all limits, beyond all time,
endless, engaging, ever-present Love.

---

2. Sing one verse of *God of the Bible* (*More Voices* #28), before
   each section and after the prayer is complete. Or sing the first
   verse of *Holy, Holy, Holy, Lord God Almighty* (*Voices United*
   #315) or a verse of *Praise Our Maker* (*Voices United* #316)
   before each section.

Sunday between May 29 and June 4 inclusive (if after Trinity Sunday)

Proper 4 [9]

LECTIONARY READINGS

1 Samuel 3:1–10	**or**	Deuteronomy 5:12–15
Psalm 139:1–6,13–18		Psalm 81:1–10

2 Corinthians 4:5–12
Mark 2:23—3:6

Jesus does not go by the letter of the law but by the spirit of law.

Not by the letter of the law but by the spirit of the law.
Not the letter but the spirit.
We give thanks for employers who employ immigrants who
have the right skills but no formal qualifications.
We give thanks for employers who give opportunities to those
who are challenged mentally and physically and who modify
the workplace accordingly.
We give thanks for police officers who understand that a
warning may be more of a deterrent than a fine or formal
charge.
We give thanks for doctors and dentists who waive scheduled
fees for those without the financial means for treatment.
We give thanks to government officials who take the time to
explain forms to elderly and confused persons.
Jesus was a spirit person.
He shows us the spirit way.

Not the letter but the spirit.
We give thanks for drug companies that charge sufferers in
developing countries less for HIV/AIDS drugs than those in
developed nations.
We give thanks for those who give priority medical treatment
to the most vulnerable.
We give thanks for nurses and others who bend the rules so
that family members can stay with patients after visiting
hours are over.

We give thanks for animal doctors who realize that for some
owners the loss of a dog or cat means the loss of their best
friend.
We give thanks for medical staff who assist a patient to end
their life when it has become merely existence.
We pray for sick, dying, and bereaved persons in our own
families and in the church family *(time of silent reflection)*.
Jesus was a spirit person.
He shows us the spirit way.

Not the letter but the spirit.
We give thanks for churches that have given shelter to persons
seeking political asylum.
We give thanks for churches that welcome the youngest to
Holy Communion and provide elements that are neither
addictive nor physically harmful *(non-alcoholic wine,
gluten-free bread)*.
We give thanks for members who risk arrest and
imprisonment by protesting against policies that are
harmful or discriminatory. And we give thanks for faith
communities that support them.
We give thanks for Christian communities overseas that break
national laws in order to worship, serve, and promote the
way of Jesus Christ.
Jesus was a spirit person.
He shows us the spirit way.

Not the letter but the spirit.
We give thanks for those who have helped us by going the
extra mile.
We give thanks for teachers who worked with us after school
hours ended.
We give thanks for fellow workers who let us learn from
mistakes that should have cost us our job.
We give thanks for friends who stood with us when we let
them down, by word or by action.
We give thanks for family members who shouldered the anger
or rejection that was ours alone.
Not by the letter of the law but by the spirit of the law.
Jesus was a spirit person.
He shows us the spirit way.

Another Way

1. Use the Gospel story – Jesus sees a man who is paralyzed and heals him – as the prayer focus.

 You care for us, O God; you care for our world.
Where farmers face ruin as a result of disease among
livestock, your care is found among patient researchers
and diligent veterinarians *(current national or international
situation).*
When an epidemic rages, your care is found among hard
working health officials and dedicated nursing staff and
doctors *(current national or international situation).*
Where poverty is a fact of life, your care shines out as people
are given lasting work and a sound home. We pray for
(current national or international situation).
Where superstition casts its long shadow, your care is among
those who show there is no reason to fear.
Jesus identified need, and then acted.
Are we alert to need, and will we act?

 **You care for us, O God; you care for those who bring
understanding and hope.**
When a friendship is on the rocks, your care is found in the
person who will speak the truth in love, and the counsellor
who will listen without judgment.
In the shock of an unexpected diagnosis, your care is with the
doctor who takes time to explain.
In the frustration of an illness that drags on and on, your care
is with friends and family who faithfully stay beside the
sufferer.
In the hard place of loss, your care is with the person who
takes the time to listen deeply.
You care for us, O God; you care for the sick and the bereaved
(time of silent reflection).
Jesus identified need, and then acted.
Are we alert to need, and will we act?

You care for us, O God; you care for the church.
You care for those who teach our children and young people,
and help in our nursery.
Where churches are concerned for themselves first, your care
is with those who hold and make clear a wider vision.
We remember those concerned for mission projects in our
congregation *(name the persons and projects)*.
For churches that feel safest with traditional ways, your
care is with those who suggest new ways and fresh faith
partnerships.
You care for us, O God; you care for all those who are
visionaries and enablers.
Jesus identified need, and then acted.
Are we alert to need, and will we act?

You care for us, O God; you care for each one of us.
When we see a new path opening ahead of us, yet are fearful,
your care encourages us to take the first step.
When the pressures of life seem intense, your care invites us
to relax.
When the burdens of the past shadow us, your word is of
peace.
When the ties of friendship are strained, you show us the way
of understanding and reconciliation.
You care for us, O God, in all the changing scenes of life.
We will be alert to our own needs, and we will act.

2. Sing the first verse of *Jesus' Hands Were Kind Hands* (*Voices
   United* #570) or verse two of *We Are One* (*Voices United* #402)
   before each section.

Sunday between June 5 and June 11 inclusive (if after Trinity Sunday)
Proper 5 [10]

LECTIONARY READINGS
1 Samuel 8:4–11, (12–15), 16–20, (11:14–15) **or** Genesis 3:8–15
Psalm 138   Psalm 130

2 Corinthians 4:13—5:1
Mark 3:20–35

> *Jesus asks a hard question of the teachers of the law:*
> *"How can Satan drive out Satan?"*

There are tough questions to be answered.
Why are the nations of the world not able to forget their
   differences?
We pray for perseverance along the way to peace *(current*
   international area of conflict).
How can the voices of the homeless and the poor be heard
   by the powerful?
We pray for those seeking support for women's shelters and
   the food banks of *(own town/city).*
We pray for those who go the hard route of lobbying political
   leaders and protesting without violence.
Christ stands beside the poor, the innocent, and the
vulnerable.
In our efforts to support those for whom we pray,
Where does our Christian approach lead us?

There are tough questions to be answered.
Who are those in *(own town/city)* ***who do not have adequate***
   nutrition, clothing, or housing?
We pray for those who sleep rough, and for those who rely on
   food banks to supplement their food source.
Why are the sick and the suffering not treated on an equal
basis?
We pray for an equal distribution of diagnostic and treatment
   resources in this nation.

We pray for creative ways to diagnose and treat persons who
live in remote areas.
We think of our friends, family members, and church family
friends who are sick this morning *(time of silent reflection).*
**How can the bereaved and those suffering loss get the
comfort they need?**
We pray for family members who stay with those who mourn.
We pray for family and grief counsellors *(time of silent
reflection).*
**Christ stands with the sick, the confused, and those who
feel alone.**
In our efforts to support those for whom we pray,
Where does our Christian approach lead us?

 There are tough questions to be answered.
**Are we sure enough of our Christian faith to give it a
defining role in the way we live our life?**
We pray for ourselves as we struggle to grow as followers of '
Christ *(time of silent reflection).*
**Are we sure enough of our Christian faith to give it a
crucial role in the life of our church?** *(Time of silent
reflection.)*
We pray for the minister/pastor/priest/lay leader *(name)* of
this congregation as she/he teaches and guides us.
We pray for the leaders of our faith community as they carry
out the responsibilities entrusted to them *(time of silent
reflection).*
We pray for those who teach and inspire and stay alongside
young persons *(time of silent reflection).*
**Are we willing to give sacrificially, so that persons we do
not know in other countries will be supported and helped
in the way of Christ?**
We pray for those supported by our mission funds *(time of
silent reflection).*
**Christ stands with the faith community in struggle and
certainty.**
In our efforts to support those for whom we pray,
Where does our Christian approach lead us?

*There are tough questions to be answered. Questions we
can answer only in our heart of hearts.*
*What does our Christian faith call us to do at home, at
church, in our suffering world?*
(Time of silent reflection.)
Why can we not achieve those things we dream of doing?
We ask for clarity of purpose and the will to venture out.
We ask for good friends to support us; friends who are willing
to be straightforward with us.
How can we overcome the obstacles that bedevil us?
We pray for the courage to speak the truth without fear.
We pray for patient endurance in the face of envy and
criticism.
**We rejoice that Christ stands with those who take the risky
but faithful road.**
**Will our Christian discipleship lead us to the life that
satisfies spirit, heart, and mind?**

Another Way

1. Jesus poses the questions, "Who is my mother, and who are
    my brothers and sisters?"

*Questions from Jesus: "Who is my mother? And who are
my brothers and sisters?"*
A question for us: "Who is part of my family?"
The young boy sitting in the rubble of a city devastated by an
earthquake looks at you and asks, "Are you my mother?"
A political prisoner languishing in jail with no hope of release
asks the question, "Are you my brother?"
A young mother earning minimum wage, trying desperately to
keep her young family together, looks at you and asks, "Are
you my sister?"
A downhearted man who has retrained but has been unable to
find any work asks the question, "Are you my brother?"
Loving God,
broaden our understanding of family.

Questions from Jesus: "Who is my mother? And who are
my brothers and sisters?"
A question for us: "Who is part of my family?"
A newcomer to the faith community anxious to feel
   acceptance among many strangers, asks the question, "Are
   you my mother?"
A young man who has been let down by his best friend asks
   the question, "Are you my brother?"
A homebound person who longs for a visit and for news of
   "her" church asks the question, "Are you my sister?"
A young woman in Bangladesh whose health clinic has asked
   for support from the mission fund of the national church
   asks the question, "Are you my brother?"
Loving God,
broaden our understanding of family.

Follow the same pattern for the other sections.

2. Creatively use the song *Who Is My Mother? (More Voices*
   #178) as part of this prayer.

Sunday between June 12 and June 18 inclusive (if after Trinity Sunday)

Proper 6 [11]

LECTIONARY READINGS

1 Samuel 15:34—16:13 **or** Ezekiel 17:22–24
Psalm 20 Psalm 92:1–4, 12–15

2 Corinthians 5:6–10, (11–13), 14–17
Mark 4:26–34

Parables of seeds.

The seed must be planted in order for your Realm/ Kingdom to come, O God:
Planted by small groups working quietly but effectively for peace;
Planted by neighbourhood groups who provide start-up money and assistance to newcomers searching for fresh skills and jobs;
Planted by those with a new and inclusive vision who are dissatisfied with the political order;
Planted by those ignored and discriminated against who are banding together to bring change.
We pray for *(local and national "seed" initiatives)*.
The seed is planted, the plant is watered, and the fruit is harvested.
God's Realm/Kingdom will come.

The plant must be watered in order for your Realm/ Kingdom to come, O God:
Watered by those who speak out for the rights of working people and advocate on their behalf;
Watered by those who stay beside the depressed and lonely and give them hope;
Watered by those who encourage and support the sick and troubled;
Watered by the gentle presence of persons who hear the anger

and grief of the bereaved *(time of silent reflection)*.
We pray for *(groups and individuals who "water")*.
The seed is planted, the plant is watered, and the fruit is harvested.
God's Realm/Kingdom will come.

The fruit must be harvested in order for your Realm/ Kingdom to come O God:
Harvested by those who have spiritual hunger and will not rest until that hunger is satisfied;
Harvested by those who stand among the faithful and are not afraid to speak of their beliefs;
Harvested by those who believe in the local church and give and work for its healthy growth;
Harvested by those whose vision is broad enough to take in the wider work of the church and its partners overseas *(time of silent reflection)*.
We pray for *(those groups and individuals who "harvest")*.
The seed is planted, the plant is watered, and the fruit is harvested.
God's Realm/Kingdom will come.

Count us in, Loving God, among those who plant and water and harvest the good seed.
Count us in as individuals, count us in as a community of your faithful people.

Another Way

1. Sing one verse of *When Seed Falls on Good Soil* (*Voices United* #503) after each section.

2. Use the parable of the mustard seed as the theme of the prayer.

The mustard seed.
The smallest of beginnings.
A handful of voters peacefully protest against election fraud.
The mustard seed.
A group of friends start a co-operative kitchen.
The mustard seed.
A few unemployed people start a support group.
The mustard seed.
Some tenants band together to get fire regulations
   implemented.
From the tiny seed,
A mighty tree will grow.

The mustard seed.
The smallest of beginnings.
Political representatives are lobbied to ensure that persons
   who are physically challenged have access to all restaurant
   washrooms.
The mustard seed.
The parent of a child who has to wait several months for an
   operation writes persistently to the hospital board.
The mustard seed.
The spouse of a person who has Alzheimer's disease gets
   together with others to form a daycare.
The mustard seed.
The family member of patient who is terminally ill in hospital
   works with others to provide a hospice.
From the tiny seed,
A mighty tree will grow.

Follow the same pattern for the other sections.

Sunday between June 19 and June 25 inclusive (if after Trinity Sunday)
Proper 7 [12]

LECTIONARY READINGS
1 Samuel 17:(1a, 4–11, 19–23), 32–49 **and** Psalm 9:9–20
or Job 38:1–11 **and** Psalm 107:1–3, 23–32
or 1 Samuel 17:57—18:5, 10–16 **and** Psalm 133

2 Corinthians 6:1–13
Mark 4:35–41

Jesus calms the storm on the lake.

We search for your calming presence in our troubled world, Loving God.
We find it among those who care for the homeless in *(local town)*, *(nearby major city)*, and Mumbai *(or other world city)*.
We find it among those who persist in peacemaking in the Middle East and in *(area of current unrest)*.
We find it among those who diligently look after the children of those who work outside the home.
We find it among those who encourage and support women and men who are unexpectedly unemployed.
We find it where prisoners are not simply punished but given help to turn their lives around.
Our world is crying out for a peaceful presence.
Where the storm rages,
make us instruments of your peace.

We search for your calming presence where trouble and distress are found, Loving God.
We find it where those who have lost a livelihood or been made homeless in *(current natural or man-made disaster)* are reassured through practical help.
We find it where medical or nursing staff are supported in stressful times.
We find it where the enraged and the mentally sick receive the gentle care they deserve.
We find it where the fearful dying are given the resources they need.

We find it where those who mourn find a stillness that
  consoles.
*In silence we offer to God the names of those who are suffering or
  afraid.*
The suffering are crying out for a peaceful presence.
Where the storm rages,
make us instruments of your peace.

 We search for your calming presence in the church,
  Loving God.
We find it in spiritual exercise and the inspiration of prayer.
We find it as we offer songs of praise in our community
  worship services.
We find it as your Word speaks to our personal distress and
  unease.
We find it as your Word calls us from dead ends to a life that is
  fulfilling and faithful.
We find it as our horizons widen to take in the needs of faith
  communities worldwide.
Our church is a fellowship where peace is found and
  created.
Where the storm rages,
make us instruments of your peace.

 We search for your calming presence within ourselves,
  Loving God.
We find it in a desire to forget self-interest and live generously.
We find it as we face our destructive ways and put them
  behind us.
We find it as we learn from our mistakes.
We find it as we reach out to those who speak the truth to us,
  and we open to their insights.
We find it as we work with others to bring peace to persons
  who are troubled and oppressed.
We find it in our recognition of talents we hardly thought
  were ours.
Count us among those open to your peaceful Spirit,
  Loving God.
Count us among those who bring the peaceful spirit of
  Jesus Christ into the world,
when and where the storm rages.

Another Way

1. Sing a verse from one of the many songs or hymns of peace before, during, and/or after each section of the prayer. For example, *Make Me a Channel of Your Peace* (*Voices United* #684) or *May the God of Peace* (*More Voices* #224). Or use the first verse of *Come and Find the Quiet Centre* (*Voices United* #374) as a prelude to the prayer.

2. Focus the prayer on the word peace.

In our world, peace.
Peace.
We pray for peace to come to *(current area of conflict).*
Peace.
We pray for the peace that comes when children are cared for with love. We think of *(current need for childcare).*
Peace.
We pray for the peace that is present when the homeless find a home. We think of *(current local or overseas need).*
Peace.
We pray for peace among those who are looking for a job. We think of *(current local need).*
God's peace,
the peace that Jesus experienced and brought to others.

Among the suffering, peace.
Peace.
We pray for the peace that comes when a friend or loved one makes contact after a long while. We think of *(current local situation).*
Peace.
We pray for the relief of peace as fearful men and women have their medical diagnoses confirmed.
Peace.
We pray for the peace that comes when the disturbed or mentally sick get the necessary treatment. We think of *(current need for the treatment of mental illness).*
Peace.

We pray for the peace that comes when the chronically sick get the pain relief they need.

Peace.

We pray for peace for those who are dying, and those who have been bereaved *(time of silent reflection)*.

God's peace,

the peace that Jesus experienced and brought to others.

Use the same pattern for the other sections.

Sunday between June 26 and July 2 inclusive
Proper 8 [13]

LECTIONARY READINGS
2 Samuel 1:1, 17–27
Psalm 130
  or   Wisdom of Solomon 1:13–15, 2:23–24
  and   Lamentations 3:23–33   **or**   Psalm 30

2 Corinthians 8:7–15
Mark 5:21–43

The healing of Jairus' daughter and the woman who touched the hem of Jesus' cloak in faith.

There seems no ground for hope, but have faith.
We pray for military personnel who suffer from post-traumatic stress disorder.
We pray for those who struggle to escape conditions of poverty and oppression in their homeland *(area of current need)*.
We pray for children who have lost parents to HIV/AIDS and rely on older siblings and grandparents to bring them up.
We pray for those who have lost their homes through flooding *(or other natural disaster)* in *(area of current need)*.
We pray for those who have just been released from prison.
We pray for elderly persons who have just moved from a long-cherished home.
Have faith.
We will work and pray for the reality of a restored and faithful life.

There seems no ground for hope, but have faith.
We pray for those who have lost their financial independence.
We pray for those who cannot find out the reason for their pain.
We pray for those who through accident or conflict have lost their mobility.
We pray for those who are unexpectedly sick.

We pray for those who are dying and afraid.
We pray for those who have been suddenly bereaved (*time of silent reflection*).
Have faith.
We will work and pray for the reality of a restored and faithful life.

There seems no ground for hope, but have faith.
We pray for those who have no time or interest in a spiritual life.
We pray for those who say, "The church is dying."
We pray for those who hang back from giving their time and talents to God's work.
We pray for those who equate the faith community with the building.
We pray for those who are unable to envision a worldwide, joyful, yet needy church.
Have faith.
We will work and pray for the reality of a restored and faithful life.

There are times when our faith is weak,
When our trust in a good friend or a loved one is lost;
When work is unfulfilling, or attending a local social group is a chore;
When our life's path is strewn with obstacles;
When our prayer life is dry and our spiritual searching yields no results;
When there seems no one to turn to in our need.
The prospects seem dim but
we believe, and we will work and pray for the reality of a restored and faithful life.

Another Way

1. Sing *Behold, Behold, I Make All Things New* (*More Voices* #115), or verse two of *O for a Thousand Tongues to Sing* (*Voices United* #326) before each section.

2. Focus a fully responsive prayer on healing.

Healing will happen
when financial realities are faced.
Healing will happen
when the nature of an illness is made clear.
Healing will happen
when the instructions of the medical professional are followed
  carefully.
Healing will happen
when a person believes that change is possible.
Healing will happen
when workplaces and restaurants are made accessible to all.
Healing will happen
when the bereaved are allowed the time they need to grieve.
There will be healing,
and life will be restored.

Healing will happen to us
when we face our fears and guilt.
Healing will happen to us
as trust in a loved one returns.
Healing will happen to us
as fulfilling work is found.
Healing will happen to us
when the way ahead becomes clear.
Healing will happen to us
as the Spirit gently touches our spiritual life.
There will be healing,
and life will be restored.

Use the same pattern for the other sections.

Sunday between July 3 and July 9 inclusive
Proper 9 [14]

LECTIONARY READINGS

2 Samuel 5:1–5, 9–10   **or**   Ezekiel 2:1–5
Psalm 48   Psalm 123

2 Corinthians 12:2–10
Mark 6:1–13

Jesus is rejected in his hometown.

Rejection is tough to take.
Job seekers who are turned down for a position know this.
Young persons who run up against inflexible immigration
    rules are crushed by this.
Persons who seek political office or leadership in social
    organizations know this.
The hungry who have children to feed and no resources to
    offer are achingly aware of this.
We pray for *(current persons and situations).*
The rejected are our bothers and sisters.
We will stand with them.

Rejection is tough to take.
Ignored newcomers to a sports or social group know this.
Boys and girls who want to make friends but are turned down
    are hurt by this.
Lovers denied the relationship they seek feel this deeply.
Sick persons who have to wait to see a specialist know this.
Chronically ill persons whose friends don't visit experience
    this.
The dying whose friends cannot bring themselves to visit
    know this *(time of silent reflection).*
The bereaved who are ignored after the first few weeks of loss
    are aware of this.
The rejected are our bothers and sisters.
We will stand with them.

Rejection is tough to take.
Newcomers to the church who are disregarded know this.

Volunteers who work long and hard yet receive no thanks or words of appreciation feel this.
Members who voice valid criticism of leaders are aware of this.
Visionaries who look to new ways of worship and linking with other faith communities know this.
The rejected are our bothers and sisters.
We will stand with them.

 Rejection is a part of the experience of each one of us.
We feel rejection as we suggest fresh ways of being and doing.
We feel rejection in the family circle when an offer of help is turned down.
We feel rejection at work when our suggestions for improved ways of working are not taken seriously.
We feel rejection as we seek justice for the vulnerable in our locality.
We feel rejection when we are ignored, talked down to, or not heard (*time of silent reflection*).
We will identify our feelings of rejection, work with the wise ones, and put rejection behind us, as Jesus did.

Another Way

1. **Sing the chorus of *Spirit, Open My Heart* (*More Voices* #79) after each section.**

2. **Base the prayer on the sending out of the twelve disciples.**

 Go out in hope.
Young persons will find the understanding and the listening ear they seek.
Go out in hope.
The rejected will be able to talk over their feelings with a loved one.
Go out in hope.
Those persons unexpectedly sick will get the treatment they need.
Go out in hope.

The dying will know the presence of their friends (*time of silent reflection*).
Go out in hope
The bereaved will find the support they seek.
Hope is not wishful thinking.
Faithful hope leads to a new reality.

 Go out in hope.
People are seeking a renewed spiritual life.
Go out in hope.
The ultimate questions – *Where have I come from? How shall I live a fulfilling life? What happens when I die?* – are waiting for a Christian answer.
Go out in hope.
So many, near and far, need the compassion of Christ.
Go out in hope
of a faith community that seeks renewal (*time of silent reflection*).
Hope is not wishful thinking.
Faithful hope leads to a new reality.

Use the same pattern for the other sections.

Sunday between July 10 and July 16 inclusive

Proper 10 [15]

LECTIONARY READINGS

2 Samuel 6:1–5, 12b–19   **or**   Amos 7:7–15
Psalm 24   Psalm 85:8–13

Ephesians 1:3–14
Mark 6:14–29

The death of John the Baptizer.

A faithful prophet will be heeded and honoured:
The prophet who speaks out for peaceful protest when others
  are calling for violence;
The prophet who insists that oil companies reduce carbon
  emissions even though that will lead to less employment and
  lower profits;
The prophet who works for political freedom even though it
  will mean imprisonment;
The prophet who sacrifices family life, security, a worthwhile
  job, even life itself, for what she/he believes.
We will listen to the prophets.
We will be prophets in our own time and situation.

A faithful prophet will be heeded and honoured.
The prophet calls for an end to suffering.
"No child on this planet shall go hungry," is the prophetic
  message.
"Every refugee woman will be protected from abuse," is the
  prophetic message.
"The amount you earn will not decide how quickly you are
  diagnosed and treated," is the prophetic message.
"The old and infirm will be treated with understanding and
  respect," is the prophetic message.
"The sick young ones will always be able to have their parents
  with them," is the prophetic message.
"The dying will be given dignity," is the prophetic message.
"Those who have lost loved ones will be given the time they

need to express anger and loss," is the prophetic message
(*time of silent reflection*).
We will listen to the prophets.
We will be prophets in our own time and situation.

 A faithful prophet will be heeded and honoured.
Prophets are needed in the church.
They speak out to welcome in a practical way gays and
lesbians, physically and mentally challenged persons.
They speak out for the imperative to try out new forms of
worship and song.
They speak out for the need to listen for God's Word in books
other than the Bible.
They speak out for the struggle to put the Good News into
a context that is radically different from first-century
Palestine or 20th-century North America.
They speak out for a renewed mission that begins in the
backyard of the local church, extends into the local
community, and blossoms into a worldwide enterprise.
We will listen to the prophets.
We will be prophets in our own time and situation.

 Do we have the qualities to be effective prophets?
Are we willing to speak out when others are afraid?
Are we willing to prophesy without counting the cost?
Are we willing to lose friends and antagonize family members
through our prophesies?
Are we willing to jeopardize our work situation or our
position in a social group by saying the words that need to
be said?
Have we thought about prophetic actions that speak louder
than words?
**You challenge us, Just God, to be prophets in our own
day and generation.**

Another Way

1. Sing the chorus of *Go Make a Diff'rence* (*More Voices* #209)
   after each section. Or sing *What Does the Lord Require of You*
   (*Voices United* #701) before each section.

2. Focus the prayer on responding to the prophet's challenge.

A prophet like John is not afraid to speak out.
The prophet will speak of the children denied food and
adequate housing in (*area of current need*).
The prophet will speak against the muzzling of political
opinions in (*area of current repression*).
The prophet will speak as the voice of the poorest and the
downtrodden.
The prophet will speak out against corrupt and self-serving
leaders.
Listen to the prophet's voice.
Respond to the prophet's challenge.

A prophet like John is not afraid to speak out.
Where church members are content with worship and service
in traditional patterns, the prophet will speak of trying out
fresh ways.
Where the church building is seen as the only place for study
and worship, the prophet will call members to new locations
in the local community.
Where the Bible is seen as the holy book above all others,
the prophet will direct faith community members to
the scriptures of other faith groups, and to wise secular
writings.
Where the conventional *mother, father, children* family unit is
seen as central to church life, the prophet will encourage the
care of alternative family configurations and single persons.
Listen to the prophet's voice.
Respond to the prophet's challenge.

Use the same pattern for the other sections.

Sunday between July 17 and July 23 inclusive
Proper 11 [16]

LECTIONARY READINGS

| 2 Samuel 7:1–14a | **or** | Jeremiah 23:1–6 |
| Psalm 89:20–37 | | Psalm 23 |

Ephesians 2:11–22
Mark 6:30–34, 53–56

Jesus takes the disciples away for a time of relaxation, but the crowds locate him and he responds to their needs.

Jesus needed a time of peace and relaxation, and so do we.
Time to reflect quietly on the needs of our troubled world and how we might respond to those needs.
Time for thankfulness for a regular source of food, for family and friends that love us, and for the rain and sunshine that nourish our life-giving earth.
Time to put behind us the everyday routines and welcome fresh insights and new friends.
Time to simply *be*, without thought of how much we have to do or achieve (*time of silent reflection*).
**Breathe your Spirit into our busy lives, Loving God,
and we will know your peace, your all-embracing peace.**

Jesus needed a time of peace and relaxation, and so do we.
As we relax we become aware of the wonder of the body and its amazing renewal as we sleep.
As we relax we remember those who find it difficult to get to sleep, and those for whom pain is an everyday fact of life.
As we relax we welcome fresh thoughts and inspirations.
As we relax we are aware of those who are sick and troubled, for whom peace is a rare commodity.
As we relax we bring to mind those who have lost loved ones, and persons for whom a time of quiet is disturbing (*time of silent reflection*).
**Breathe your Spirit into our busy lives, Loving God,
and we will know your peace, your all-embracing peace.**

Jesus needed a time of peace and relaxation, and so do we.
We need peace in the church:
The peace that comes through prayer, the familiar songs sung
    with others, and the well-loved Bible stories;
The peace that comes through swopping stories and news
    with good friends in a friendly place;
The peace that comes through appreciating family members
    and friends who have worshipped and served this faith
    community over many years;
The peace that comes through reflecting on how the
    challenges of the faith community may be met in coming
    months (*time of reflection*).
The peace that comes through meeting needs in the local
    community and beyond.
Breathe your Spirit into our busy lives, Loving God,
and we will know your peace, your all-embracing peace.

Jesus needed a time of peace and relaxation, and so do we.
Each one of us needs peace.
The peace that is ours as we apologize for a word or action
    that has hurt or caused trouble.
The peace that is ours when we offer or accept forgiveness.
The peace that is ours as we face up to and accept a limitation
    of mind or body.
The peace that is ours as we read a new book, embark on
    a new area of learning, or engage in a sport or exercise
    program.
The peace that is ours as we change a life's direction that has
    been unhealthy or unfulfilling.
The peace that is ours as we commit to a new endeavour that
    brings joy or peace to other people (*time of reflection*).
Breathe your Spirit into our busy lives, Loving God,
and we will know your peace, your all-embracing peace.

Another Way

1. Slow the whole prayer down and allow more time for
   reflection.

Jesus needed a time of peace and relaxation, and so do we.
Peace.
We relax and become aware of the wonder of our body and its
amazing renewal as we sleep.
We relax and remember those who find it difficult to get to
sleep, and those for whom pain is an everyday fact of life
(*time of silent reflection*).
Peace.
We relax and welcome fresh thoughts and words of
inspiration.
We relax and become aware of those who are sick and
troubled, for whom peace is a rare commodity (*time of silent
reflection*).
Peace.
We relax and bring to mind those who have lost loved ones,
and persons for whom a time of quiet is disturbing (*time of
silent reflection*).
**Breathe your Spirit into our busy lives, Loving God,
and we will know your peace, your all-embracing peace.**

Jesus needed a time of peace and relaxation, and so do we.
Each one of us needs peace.
The peace that is ours as we apologize for a word or action
that has hurt or caused trouble.
The peace that is ours when we offer or accept forgiveness
(*time of silent reflection*).
Peace.
The peace that is ours as we face up to and accept a limitation
of mind or body.
The peace that is ours as we read a new book, embark on
a new area of learning, or engage in a sport or exercise
program (*time of silent reflection*).
Peace.
The peace that is ours as we change a life's direction that has
been unhealthy or unfulfilling.
The peace that is ours as we commit to a new endeavour that
brings joy or peace to others (*time of reflection*).
**Breathe your Spirit into our busy lives, Loving God,
and we will know your peace, your all-embracing peace.**

2. Sing a verse from one of the many songs or hymns of peace before, during, and/or after each section of the prayer. For example, sing *Make Me a Channel of Your Peace* (*Voices United* #684) or *May the God of Peace* (*More Voices* #224). Or use the first verse of *Come and Find the Quiet Centre* (*Voices United* #374) as a prelude to the prayer.

Sunday between July 24 and July 30 inclusive
Proper 12 [17]

LECTIONARY READINGS

2 Samuel 11:1–15	**or**	2 Kings 4:42–44
Psalm 14		Psalm 145:10–18

Ephesians 3:14–21
John 6:1–21

The miracle of the loaves and fishes. All ate as much as they wanted and were satisfied.

 The provision of good food is a challenge, Living God.
We pray for those men and women, boys and girls of our rich
and fertile planet who go to bed without having had enough
to eat *(current area of famine or special need)*.
We pray for farmers with weather challenges, who worry
about the timing of the harvest or the quality of the crops.
We pray for those who are unable to control their eating and
drinking and have an unhealthy weight.
We pray for those who purposely restrict the food they eat to
the detriment of their health.
We pray for the agencies *(names)* that make sure that our food
is safe to eat *(time of silent reflection)*.
Our wish is your wish, Living God,
that all will eat as much as they need and be satisfied.

 The provision of good food is a challenge, Living God.
We pray for those who have eating disorders and for those
who are addicted to drugs or alcohol.
We pray for new mothers who are unable to supply their
babies with milk, and for those who support them.
We pray for dieticians and medical personnel who give advice
on what to eat and drink.
We pray for those for whom the death of a loved one has
affected their appetite or eating pattern.
We pray for the sick and bereaved in our families and the
church family *(time of silent reflection)*.

Our wish is your wish, Living God,
that all will eat as much as they need and be satisfied.

The provision of good food is a challenge, Living God.
We pray for the members of this church who unfailingly
    supply soup, meals, and baking for the different functions of
    this faith community.
We pray for those who are provided with food through the
    efforts of the local church, or through its support of a
    community food bank.
As Jesus provided food not just for the body but for the mind
    and soul, so we pray for the clergy *(names)* and other
    teachers *(names)* who through sermons and study groups
    satisfy the learning appetites of the faith community.
We pray for mission programs that enable farmers and fishers
    in other countries to sustainably harvest more crops or fish
    (time of silent reflection).
Our wish is your wish, Living God,
that all will eat as much as they need and be satisfied.

The provision of good food is a challenge, Living God.
We give thanks for those so frequent times when the food we
    need has been readily available for us.
We give thanks for the members of our families who are the
    cooks and meal-makers.
We give thanks for the breadwinners in our families, and for
    those who through their vegetable and fruit gardens and
    community lots supply family food needs.
We give thanks for those who meet our spiritual and
    intellectual needs, and those who help us use the power of
    the Internet to challenge injustice and oppression.
We give thanks for Jesus, the Bread of Life *(time of silent
    reflection).*
**We rejoice, Living God, that we are able to eat as much
as we need and are satisfied.**

Another Way

1. Sing *God Bless to Us Our Bread* (*More Voices* #193) before
   each section. Verse two of *When I Needed a Neighbour*
   (*Voices United* #600) is also particularly appropriate.

2. Focus the prayer on praising God as Sustainer.

You nourish us, Creator God, and we thank you.
We thank you for the food that sustains us and the drink that
   is essential to our well-being.
We thank you for those who produce, pack, and transport
   our food.
We thank you for those who alert us to the dangers of eating
   unhealthy food, or carrying too much weight.
We thank you for those who alert us to the needs of boys,
   girls, women, and men the world over who are poorly
   nourished.
May our thanks take the practical form of support for farmers
   and local food producers, the dietary visionaries, and the
   agencies that feed the world's poor and teach and finance
   improved farming methods.
God, Creator and Sustainer of us all,
we praise you.

You nourish us Creator God, and we thank you.
We thank you for dieticians and others who show how good
   nutrition is the way to good health.
We thank you for meal-making and housekeeping staff in
   hospitals.
We thank you for those who research food products and
   determine which foods make for health.
We pray for those who are unhealthy and for those who seek
   to bring them back to good health.
We pray for those who have lost loved ones (*time of silent
   reflection*).
May our thanks take the practical form of *support* for health
   personnel;

may it take the form of *example* when consuming food and
   drink;
and may it take the form of *vigilance* to alert us to the dangers
   of too much salt and sugar, or additives, in our food.
God, Creator and Sustainer of us all,
we praise you.

Use the same pattern for the other sections.

Sunday between July 31 and August 6 inclusive
Proper 13 [18]

LECTIONARY READINGS

2 Samuel 11:26—12:13a   **or**   Exodus 16:2–4, 9–15
Psalm 51:1–12   Psalm 78:23–29

Ephesians 4:1–16
John 6:24–35

Jesus tells the people that he is the bread of life.

What does our world hunger for?
There is a hunger for the spirit of Christ in our world:
Agencies that are committed to feeding the hungry and
    protecting the vulnerable in our area;
Groups that are committed to speaking up for released
    prisoners and those in prison for religious or political
    beliefs;
Persons who are committed to sharing their resources with
    the poor and those without hope;
Political leaders who are not afraid to provide money to those
    in other countries who lack food, shelter, and security – the
    basics of life that we take for granted.
"I am the bread of life," said Jesus.
"Those who come to me will never be hungry."

What do the suffering hunger for?
There is a hunger for the spirit of Christ among the suffering:
Where the unemployed are supported and encouraged, the
    spirit of Christ is there.
Where sick persons are received warmly and treated promptly,
    the spirit of Christ is there.
Where there is sharing of childcare and work in the home, the
    spirit of Christ is there.
Where the opinions of children are taken seriously, their joys
    celebrated, their concerns heard, the spirit of Christ is there.
Where the bereaved find a friend who listens patiently over
    days and weeks, the spirit of Christ is there.
We pray for those we know and those in the church family

who are in need today *(time of silent reflection).*
"I am the bread of life," said Jesus.
"Those who come to me will never be hungry.*"*

What does the church hunger for?
There is a hunger for the spirit of Christ in the church:
The spirit of Christ is with those whose joy and enthusiasm
    for the Christian way is communicated in worship.
The spirit of Christ is with those who will not rest with fixed
    belief statements and biblical certainty.
The spirit of Christ is with those who refuse to give in to the
    spirit of materialism that stalks our culture.
The spirit of Christ is with those who have a broad vision of
    church and give generously to people they will never know
    in countries they will never visit.
"I am the bread of life," said Jesus.
"Those who come to me will never be hungry."

What do we hunger for, each one of us?
We hunger for the spirit of Jesus Christ:
For his certain trust in the Holy One;
For the vision and self-confidence he displayed;
For his willingness to confront unthinking leaders;
For the certainty of his lifestyle choices;
For his refusal to take the easy way out;
For his compassionate eye, always on the lookout for the
    downtrodden and rejected.
"I am the bread of life," said Jesus.
"Those who come to me will never be hungry."

Another Way

1. Sing *Bread of Life, Feed My Soul* (*More Voices* #194) – either
   verse one after each section, or verses one and two after
   the World section, verses three and four after the Suffering
   section, and verse five after the Church section. Repeat verses
   one and two at the end of the prayer.

2. Engage the congregation in a dialogue about hunger
   and then use the prayer from Proper 14 as a guide to
   crafting a prayer. Make the point that hunger is a basic
   human condition and ask about times when individuals
   in the congregation have been hungry. Then broaden the
   discussion to include those in our world who are hungry
   right now.

   Talk of the word hunger as it refers to "deep
   longing" – a hunger for shelter for the transients in
   our community, or a hunger for improved daycare
   facilities. In the Suffering section, consider the hunger
   for improved emergency treatment that might be
   an issue in your community, or a deep hunger for a
   hospice where the dying are treated with dignity.
   The Church section might reveal a hunger for people
   to sing the old hymns more often, or for an outreach
   study group to be held in a local library or store.

   It will be useful to have two persons involved in this
   dialogue (as well as the congregation); one to talk
   with the congregation and another to shape a prayer.

Sunday between August 7 and August 13 inclusive
Proper 14 [19]

LECTIONARY READINGS

2 Samuel 18:5–9, 15, 31–33   **or**   1 Kings 19:4–8
Psalm 130   Psalm 34:1–8

Ephesians 4:25—5:2
˙John 6:35, 41–51

I am the bread of life.

The bread of life: food for the body, food for the soul.
The bread of life brings hope to the forgotten political
   prisoner.
We pray for (*organizations like Amnesty International*).
The bread of life brings a meal to the hungry.
We pray for (*local food bank*).
The bread of life brings relief to those who have suffered
   disaster.
We pray for (*current natural disaster*).
The bread of life brings opportunity to the unemployed.
We pray for (*current situation*).
The bread of life brings confidence to the downtrodden.
We pray for (*current situation*).
The hungry will eat and be satisfied.
We will feed them.

The bread of life: food for the body, food for the soul.
Persons who stay beside those who are miserable and
   depressed: the bread of life.
Support for those who have family members who suffer from
   dementia: the bread of life.
Strength to those who have had discouraging medical news:
   the bread of life.
Comfort to those who have suffered the loss of a cherished
   dream or a loved one: the bread of life (*time of reflection*).
The hungry will eat and be satisfied.
We will feed them.

The bread of life: food for the body, food for the soul.
Bread broken, wine poured out; the community of Jesus comes
together at Holy Communion and is thankful.
Food and fellowship shared at table, help offered, troubles
deeply heard; the community of Jesus eats, listens, and is
thankful.
Challenges in the local community faced and help offered;
the community of Jesus works with others and they are
thankful.
Gifts given for mission work; the community of Jesus takes
responsibility for the work of the wider church and many in
this country and overseas are thankful.
The hungry will eat and be satisfied.
We will feed them.

The bread of life: food for the body, food for the soul.
The bread of life inspires us to find our spiritual path and
persevere on it.
The bread of life calls us to find the faithful leaders and follow
them.
The bread of life reminds us of the opportunities that are
before us and the talents we have to make the most of them.
The bread of life is ours as we contribute to our larger
community, our faith community, and the leisure, sports,
and social groups of which we are a part.
**The bread of life will nourish us, and enable us to
nourish others in the Way of Jesus Christ.**

Another Way

1. On a Sunday when Holy Communion is celebrated, sing *Bread
   for the Journey* (*More Voices* #202) after each section of the
   prayer.

2. Focus the prayer on Jesus as the way to eternal life.

We are called by Jesus to search for the values that last.
Lasting values.
All children have the security, food, and shelter that they
need.

Our elders treated with respect.
Those who have to resort to welfare benefits treated with
dignity.
Emergency services freely available for every person when
they need them.
A peaceful pain-free place to be for the dying.
Bereaved families provided with support and counselling (*time
of silent reflection*).
With values that will never go out of date,
we prepare for the life that has no ending, the life
embraced by God's love.

 Lasting values.
A faith community (church) continually searching for new
truth about the scriptures.
A faith community (church) rooted in the sacraments that
have sustained in the past, sustain in the present, and will
sustain in the years that lie ahead.
A faith community (church) willing to risk and adventure in
worship and in mission.
A faith community (church) unafraid to act on the prompting
of the Holy Spirit.
A faith community(church) with a vision that includes each
individual yet is global in scope.
With values that will never go out of date,
we prepare for the life that has no ending, the life
embraced by God's love.

Use the same pattern for the other sections.

Sunday between August 14 and August 20 inclusive
Proper 15 [20]

LECTIONARY READINGS

1 Kings 2:10–12, 3:3–14   **or**   Proverbs 9:1–6
Psalm 111   Psalm 34:9–14

Ephesians 5:15–20
John 6:51–58

The bread I will give you for the life of the world is my flesh.

Renewed life for the world. Jesus Christ will show us the way.
The way of Jesus Christ: justice for the poorest and the most vulnerable. We think of *(current example)*.
The way of Jesus Christ: a fair wage for those struggling to provide for their partner and family.
The way of Jesus Christ: the power seekers confronted, the traditionalists challenged *(current example)*.
The way of Jesus Christ: the spirit of the law more important than the letter of the law.
The way of Jesus Christ: the needy ones recognized and their needs joyfully met *(current example)*.
Can we see as Jesus saw? Can we hear as Jesus heard? Can we respond as Jesus responded?

Renewed life for the suffering. Jesus will show us the way.
The way of Jesus Christ: attention to the needs of children. We pray for *(children who are challenged, bullied, or have learning difficulties)*.
The way of Jesus: those most despised are noticed and helped. We pray for *(mentally sick persons, persons with HIV/AIDS)*.
The way of Jesus: the problems of those who are sick are faced up to. We pray for *(current area of medical concern)*.
We bring before God those who we know are sick *(time of silent reflection)*.
The way of Jesus: the dying and the bereaved, supported and

comforted. We pray for those who are on our minds and in our hearts *(time of silent reflection)*.
Can we see as Jesus saw? Can we hear as Jesus heard? Can we respond as Jesus responded?

Renewed life for the Church. Jesus will show us the way.
The way of Jesus: all welcomed, none turned away. We pray for *(newcomers to our faith community, learning groups, or children's activities)*.

The way of Jesus: a group of trained and committed disciples proclaiming God's Kingdom. We pray for those who are in leadership groups in our church, and those who teach and pastorally care *(current church groups)*.

The way of Jesus: up-front discussion and questioning. We pray for book study groups, and those who are working towards joining the church on profession of faith *(current church groups)*.

The way of Jesus took in those who were not of the orthodox or conventional faith. We pray for our contacts with other faith groups and other Christian churches *(specify those who meet with the local church)*.

Can we see as Jesus saw? Can we hear as Jesus heard? Can we respond as Jesus responded?

Renewed life for each one of us. Jesus will show us the way.
A way that is not compromised by the powerful or the threatening.

A way that faces temptation head-on and does not give in.

A way that is neither narrow nor restricting.

A way that listens for a call, responds to the call, and does not look back.

A way that knows the value of prayer and meditation, yet does not shrink from action.

A way that sees faith as something nurtured in a community of friends.

An intensely loving and compassionate way *(time of silent reflection)*.

Can we see as Jesus saw? Can we hear as Jesus heard? Can we respond as Jesus responded?

Another Way

1. Sing *You Are Holy* (*More Voices* #45) or verse one of *Come, My Way, My Truth* (*Voices United* #628) after each section.

2. Use the above prayer but reverse the order.

Can we see as Jesus saw? Can we hear as Jesus heard?
Can we respond as Jesus responded?

Jesus saw the poorest and the most vulnerable and met their needs. We think of (*current example*).

Jesus saw those who were struggling to get by on starvation wages and brought their plight out into the open. We think of (*current example*).

Jesus confronted the power seekers and traditionalists and challenged them to a better way (*current example*).

Jesus was taken to task by those who saw the letter of the law as more important than the spirit of the law.

Jesus recognized the needy ones as he went about his day, and joyfully met their needs (*current example*).

If we seek a renewed life for the world,
Jesus Christ will show us the way.

Use the same pattern for the other sections.

Sunday between August 21 and August 27 inclusive
Proper 16 [21]

LECTIONARY READINGS

1 Kings 8:(1, 6, 10–11), 22–30, 41–43	**or**	Joshua 24:1–2a, 14–18
Psalm 84		Psalm 34:15–22

Ephesians 6:10–20
John 6:56–69

This teaching is difficult. Who can accept it?

We need strength to follow Jesus. His words challenge us; his actions test us.
If Jesus were here today, he would speak out against those who pollute lakes and kill wildlife in order to extract oil from the earth.
If Jesus were here today, he would protest against those who build homes on good agricultural land.
If Jesus were here today, he would hold leaders to account for the killing of innocent civilians in warfare.
If Jesus were here today, he would make sure that refugees were protected and given permanent homes.
We are the hands and feet of Jesus.
Are we strong enough to do his work?

We need strength to follow Jesus. His words challenge us; his actions test us.
If Jesus were here today, he would work with the unemployed to find a fulfilling job.
If Jesus were here today, he would protest the low minimum wage that keeps working mothers from having enough time to spend with their families.
If Jesus were here today, he would make sure that all shops, restaurants, and offices were fully accessible to the physically challenged.
If Jesus were here today, he would make sure those who have

chronic pain have the medication they need delivered by the most efficient means.

If Jesus were here today, he would be the agent of peace to the dying, and a listening presence to the bereaved.
We are the hands and feet of Jesus.
Are we strong enough to do his work?

We need strength to follow Jesus. His words challenge us; his actions test us.

If Jesus were here today, he would find a way to make the Good News relevant to people focused on meeting their own needs.

If Jesus were here today, he would ask hard questions about the amount of energy and money used to preserve the buildings of the faith community.

If Jesus were here today, he would check out the latest forms of modern music and wonder why he could not hear them in church.

If Jesus were here today, he would dialogue with the leaders of other faiths, study their holy books, and discuss their statements of faith.

If Jesus were here today, he would be considered a pain in the faith community butt.
We are the hands and feet of Jesus.
Are we strong enough to do his work?

We need strength to follow Jesus. His words challenge us; his actions test us.

If Jesus were here today, it would be difficult to feel comfortable in his presence.

If Jesus were here today, we would be forced to reconsider our priorities for the use of our talent, time, and money.

If Jesus were here today, we would be carefully comparing the goals and visions of our political parties with Kingdom values.

If Jesus were here today, we would be wondering if our work and leisure activities are the ones God is calling us to be about.

If Jesus were here today, we would be laughing and crying a whole lot more in church.
We are the hands and feet of Jesus.
Are we strong enough to do his work?

Another Way

1. Sing one verse of *We Give Our Hands to You* (*More Voices* #187) before the first section and another verse after each section. Or sing verse one of *Jesus, Teacher, Brave and Bold* (*Voices United* #605) before each section.

The name of Jesus Christ is a name that resounds with justice.

It is a name that calls us to remember the suffering of political prisoners throughout the world.

It is a name that calls us to speak up for those countries left behind by the revolution in communications, and those countries where people still die of hunger.

It is a name that condemns the abuse of women and the exploitation of children (*time of silent reflection*).

It is a name that we have taken at baptism, a name that calls us to responsibility.

But this is the question that tests us:

Are our values and actions worthy of the name Christian?

The name of Jesus Christ is a name that speaks of compassion.

It is a name that will not allow the challenged ones to be ignored.

It is a name that gives hope to the sick, and comfort to the dying.

It is a name that inspires endurance in the caregivers.

It is a name that brings courage to the bereaved.

We name in silence those we know who are sick or have lost loved ones (*time of silent reflection*).

It is a name we have taken at baptism, a name that calls us to action.

But this is the question that tests us:

Are our values and actions worthy of the name Christian?

The name of Jesus Christ is the name which enfolds the church.
It·is a name shared by members diverse in outlook and
commitment.
It is a name that inspires support and listening.
It is a name that reminds us to look beyond our own
four walls.
It is a name that brings to mind the saints who have served
well in years past, and those near and dear to us who have
found peace with God (*time of silent reflection*).
It is a name we have taken at baptism, our common name in
church.
But this is the question that tests us:
Are our values and actions worthy of the name
Christian?

 The name of Jesus Christ is a treasured name for each one of us.
It is a name that we have claimed from our first faith days.
It is a name on which we have built our values.
It is a name which has governed our choices.
It is a name which has held us safe in the storms of life.
It is a name we have taken at baptism, a name we will keep
forever (*time of silent reflection*).
But this is the question that tests us:
Are our values and actions worthy of the name
Christian?

2. *Sing one verse of Welcome, Jesus, You Are Welcome (More*
   Voices #137) before each section.

Sunday between August 28 and September 3 inclusive

Proper 17 [22]

LECTIONARY READINGS

Song of Solomon 2:8–13   **or**   Deuteronomy 4:1–2, 6–9
Psalm 45:1–2, 6–9   Psalm 15

James 1:17–27
Mark 7:1–8, 14–15, 21–23

The Pharisees and teachers of the Law are stuck in the past, and Jesus calls them to put their reliance on the old traditions behind them.

If we are to be faithful, the time has come for a change:
To no longer complain about government policies without
  becoming politically active;
To be sensitive to the aspirations of the younger generation
  and help them create a society that is in tune with their
  dreams;
To find one small thing we can do to redress the balance of a
  world where some children go to bed hungry and some are
  obese;
To speak out against food ingredients that improve taste but
  compromise health;
To refuse to go along with the point of view that clean forms
  of generating power will never replace oil.
Encourage us, Loving God,
to be your agents of change.

If we are to be faithful, the time has come for a change:
To work with those who believe that prison is less a place for
  punishment and more a community where prisoners are
  fitted for a new way of life;
To speak out when a local medical group refuses to fund new
  treatments;
To be actively involved in supporting children who have
  difficulty learning, reading, or concentrating;

To visit those who are lonely at home or fearful in hospital;
To stand with those who are depressed or disillusioned;
To be a patient friend to those who have lost a loved one or
a pet (*time of silent reflection*).
Encourage us, Loving God,
to be your agents of change.

If we are to be faithful, the time has come for a change:
To believe that in these times of materialism there is also a
longing for spiritual practice;
To affirm the value of friendship and worship within a
supportive faith community;
To give thanks for the leadership up front and behind the
scenes in our church;
To realize the possibilities for health, employment, and shelter
through giving to church mission funds;
To partner with the local community in supporting the
vulnerable and lost (*time of silent reflection*).
Encourage us, Loving God,
to be your agents of change.

If we are to be faithful, the time has come for a change.
We face the need to vision for a fulfilling future.
We acknowledge the value of a relationship or friendship.
We are ready to let go of an impossible dream or a destructive
way of being.
We open to new truth, however joyful or however unpleasant
it may be.
We believe that change is possible, Loving God.
We will change.

Another Way

1. Sing *Open Our Hearts* (*More Voices* #21) before each section.
   Or sing *Take My Life and Let It Be* (*Voices United* #506) before
   the prayer and after each section.

2. Briefly dramatize the encounter of Jesus with the Pharisees
   and the teachers of the Law.

Pharisee: We see you and your disciples are eating without washing your hands in the ritually correct way. What is the meaning of this breach of God's holy law?

Jesus: You are a bunch of hypocrites. You talk about my disciples not washing their hands properly but you get out of the major family responsibility of caring for your parents by citing a tiny legal loophole and giving money to religious causes. The fact of the matter is that you know the Law, but do not work in the spirit of the law; your hearts are not in the right place. God stands with those who adhere to the *spirit* of the law.

And then pray.

Legalists say, "The rules are clear: no use of the food bank until we have gone through the vetting procedure."
Spirit of the law people say, "Take the food you need. We will fill out the paperwork later."
Legalists say, "The rules are clear: no job for you because you have served time in prison."
Spirit of the law people say, "You are qualified for the job and you have turned your life around. We will give you a chance."
Legalists say, "The rules are clear: as an employee, you cannot disclose a problem around tainted food. It's the responsibility of management."
Spirit of the law people say, "Many persons could be harmed by the contaminated product. I will blow the whistle and then it will be taken off the shelves right away." (*Time of silent reflection.*)
God's way.
Not the letter but the spirit of the law.

Legalists say, "The rules are clear: you are on the waiting list for this operation and you cannot jump up the line."
Spirit of the law people say, "You have a worsened condition, we will take you before some of the healthier patients."
Legalists say, "Our company policy is that you may only have time off to attend the funerals of close family members."
Spirit of the law people say, "By all means go to the funeral of

your friend and make up the hours some other day."
Legalists say, "Hospital policy is that only two persons are allowed in at one time to see a critically ill patient.
Spirit of the law people say, "This may be the last time you family members get to see your mother alive; don't crowd her but make sure that anyone who wants to say goodbye has the chance to do so."
We pray for those who are sick in our own family, in our friendship circle, and in our church family (*time of silent reflection*).
We pray for those who have lost loved ones (*time of silent reflection*).
God's way.
Not the letter but the spirit of the law.

Use the same pattern for the other sections.

Sunday between September 4 and September 10 inclusive

Proper 18 [23]

LECTIONARY READINGS

Proverbs 22:1–2, 8–9, 22–23   **or**   Isaiah 35:4–7a
Psalm 125   Psalm 146

James 2:1–10, (11–13), 14–17
Mark 7:24–37

Jesus goes beyond the boundaries of his native land and helps a sick child.

You are with those who go beyond boundaries, Loving God:
Politicians who refuse to toe the party line when it troubles
    their conscience;
Managers who see corruption and dishonesty and put their
    jobs on the line by speaking out;
Teachers who give tuition and counsel after school is over;
Farmers who forgo extra profit to keep livestock in healthy
    and humane conditions;
Bankers who refuse to increase gains by putting the savings of
    ordinary people at risk.
Soldiers who put their lives on the line to avoid injury to
    civilian women, men, and children.
When the boundaries are crossed, Loving God,
it is your compassionate and just country that we enter.

You are with those who go beyond boundaries, Loving God:
Engineers and computer experts who put needs in developing
    nations above financial reward in developed countries;
Doctors who give up a comfortable practice to work in a
    country where there is crying need;

Nurses who bring a breadth and concern to their jobs that
places patient needs above all else;
Childcare and daycare workers who treat each boy and girl as
if he or she were their own;
Eldercare staff who treat the men and women under their care
with unfailing courtesy and respect;
Parents who give up the chance of high salaries and promotion
to look after their children;
Funeral directors, clergy, and friends who are there for the
bereaved long after the funeral is over.
When the boundaries are crossed, Loving God,
it is your compassionate and just country that we enter.

You are with those who go beyond boundaries, Loving God:
Church members and friends who see need in their faith
community and stop at nothing to meet that need;
Church members and friends who see a way in which
the church can support persons who need help in the
neighbourhood, and work to achieve that;
Church members and friends who are willing to learn new
skills to bring the joy of the Christian adventure to young
persons in the faith community;
Young persons who have the courage to suggest different
styles of music, meditation, and prayer to the church
leaders;
Clergy who are willing to preach as authentic and
contemporary prophets.
When the boundaries are crossed, Loving God,
it is your compassionate and just country that we enter.

You are with us when we go beyond the boundaries,
Loving God:
When we refuse to go along with a popular attitude that goes
against Christian values or practice;
When we will not ignore prejudice or discrimination;
When we stand with a friend who has encountered
horrendous difficulties;
When we choose to put family responsibilities first and risk
losing our job;

When we speak out or protest in public;
When the boundaries are crossed, Loving God,
it is your compassionate and just country that we enter.

Another Way

1. Sing the first verse of *Let Us with a Gladsome Mind* (*Voices United* #234) or *Go Make a Diff'rence* (*More Voices* #209) before each section.

2. A Prayer for Labour Day

 You have given us, Living God, the ability to work and the ability to enjoy the rewards of our labour, and we thank you.
We pray for those in developing nations who work in dangerous places for low pay.
We pray for those who work in repetitive and hazardous occupations.
We pray for those who are anxious to upgrade their skills but cannot afford the time to retrain.
We pray for those who are the victims of industrial injury.
We pray for those who are subject to mental or sexual abuse in the workplace.
We pray for those who organize unions, and those who counter unsafe and unfair labour practices.
We pray for those above retirement age who have to work to pay for food and housing.
Number us among those who support those oppressed and degraded at work, and enable us to advocate for change.
We labour,
and the harvest is yours, O God.

 You have given us, Living God, the example of Jesus, who cared for the sick and dying, and we thank you.
We thank you for those who look after injured soldiers and those who help in their rehabilitation.

We thank you for those who are skilled in tending persons
   who have been injured in industrial accidents.
We thank you for skilled members of the medical profession
   who go beyond the obvious needs to bring comfort and
   healing.
We thank you for mental health professionals, who work with
   persons not understood by family or society.
We thank you for chaplains, good friends, and pastoral care
   workers, who are there for the dying.
And we remember those going through challenges of sickness,
   job loss, or bereavement today *(time of silent reflection).*
Number us among those who take the compassion of Jesus
   to heart.
We labour,
and the harvest is yours, Living God.

 You have given us, O God, the ability to make choices
   around work and leisure, and we thank you.
We thank you for useful and challenging work, and the health
   and strength to do it.
We thank you for the example of those who have opted for less
   money but a better quality of family life.
We thank you for the ability to look back over a job well done
   for many years, and for the time to volunteer and serve the
   community.
We thank you for the satisfaction of retirement, and for the
   well-earned chance to relax, and cultivate and smell the
   roses.
Number us among those who will not let work dominate our
   lives, and among those who encourage and support those
   whose working days are over.
We have laboured and we will labour,
and the harvest is yours, Living God.

Sunday between September 11 and September 17 inclusive

Proper 19 [24]

LECTIONARY READINGS

| Proverbs 1:20–33 | **or** | Isaiah 50:4–9a |
| Psalm 19 | | Psalm 116:1–9 |

James 3:1–12
Mark 8:27–38

Jesus asks the question, "Who do people say I am?"

You call us to ask the tough questions, O God.
How can the affluence of the developed nations continue to
contrast so strikingly with the needs of countries struggling
to develop their resources?
How can the need for national security be set against the
needs of individuals to travel freely and without hassle?
How can the objectives of political parties be made clear
without resorting to personal attack and storytelling?
How can the working poor get a fairer deal?
How can packaging be reduced and recycling made easier?
Challenge us, Living God,
**to pose the tough questions and to be involved in the
answers.**

You call us to ask the tough questions, O God.
Why do the authorities fail to treat the mental ill-health of
many prisoners?
Why have those students who are challenged physically and
mentally not got the full support they need?
Why do governments refuse to face the results of chronic
under-funding of the health system?
Why do some good people have such a hard time and suffer so
much?
Why does death come so suddenly to some young people, and
so slowly to those for whom life has become "existence"?
Challenge us, Living God,
**to pose the tough questions, and to be involved in the
answers.**

You call us to ask the tough questions, O God:
How is it that trivial conflicts in the faith community take up
so much time, energy, and effort?
How is it that church has remained static in a time of gigantic
advances in communications and technology?
In what ways can we make the Good News of Jesus fresh and
lively for this day and generation?
How can the crying needs of the wider community of Jesus
Christ be brought home to the local faith community?
Challenge us, Living God,
**to pose the tough questions, and to be involved in the
answers.**

You call us to ask the tough questions, O God:
Are we ready to make the change in diet that we know will
improve our health?
Are we ready to put behind us a grudge that has caused so
much pain?
How has our faith grown over the years? Are we ready to
carefully re-examine our beliefs?
Have we the confidence to create reality from our most
cherished dreams?
Where are you calling us to make your justice and your peace
come alive for other people?
Who are the needy ones in our family and friendship circle,
and how are we able to help them?
How are we able to make our local community a more
compassionate community?
**Remind us, O God, of your unfailing presence with us
over the years, and renew our hope in your
Eternal Care.**

Another Way

1. Jesus tells the crowd, "You must forget yourself, carry your
   cross, and follow me."

Who are cross-bearers in our world?

Activists who protest against the increase in the number of motor vehicles and the destruction of wildlife habitat on our fragile planet. We pray for *(names of individuals who are speaking out)*.

Campaigners for democracy in countries where one family or small group controls the government. We pray for *(names of individuals who are speaking out)*.

Relentless advocates for the downtrodden and despised. We pray for *(names of individuals who are speaking out)*.

Persistent workers for peace in countries where conflict is a way of life. We pray for *(names of individuals who are speaking out)*.

Persistent workers for industrial peace in situations where management and workers cannot get along, and corporate whistleblowers. We pray for *(names of individuals who are speaking out)*.

To bear a cross is to bear a heavy load.
Have we the strength and the endurance?

Who are cross-bearers among the suffering?

Those who speak out against drugs that are harmful are cross-bearers. We pray for *(current area of concern)*.

Those who speak up for the most vulnerable and overlooked in our society are cross-bearers. We pray for the elderly in care homes, children in hospital, street dwellers.

Those who forgo an increase in their living standards to support the poor and vulnerable.

Those who work unceasingly for the introduction of new diagnostic equipment or new ways of treating the sick are cross-bearers. We pray for *(current area of concern)*.

Those who work and volunteer in hospices, and those who participate in bereavement groups are cross-bearers. We pray for *(current area of concern)*.

We pray for those we know among family and friends who are sick and for those suffering ones in our church family *(time of reflection)*.

To bear a cross is to bear a heavy load.
Have we the strength and the endurance?

Who are the cross-bearers in the faith community?

 What crosses do we bear?

2. Sing the first verse of *When I Survey the Wondrous Cross* (*Voices United* #149) before each section, or sing the three verses of *If I Have Been the Source of Pain* (*More Voices* #76), one after each section.

Sunday between September 18 and September 24 inclusive
Proper 20 [25]

LECTIONARY READINGS

Proverbs 31:10–31   **or**   Wisdom of Solomon 1:16—2:1, 12–22
Psalm 1   *or* Jeremiah 11:18–20
and Psalm 54

James 3:13—4:3, 7–8a
Mark 9:30–37

*The disciples are arguing about who is the greatest among them.
Jesus places a child in their midst.*

Serving is the way to greatness.
Give time and money to help the most disadvantaged in our
world. We think of *(specify a current area of concern)*.
Give time and effort to speak out or work for peace. We think
of *(non-governmental agencies such as the Red Cross, that focus
on peace and support for the persecuted)*.
Give time and effort to meet a local community need. We
think of *(specify a need in your community)*.
Give time to coaching youngsters in sport or enabling them to
have fun together.
Offer your assistance for leadership or work in a group you
belong to.
**"Whoever wants to be first
must be the servant of all."**

Serving is the way to greatness.
Serving those who are housebound and need help cooking and
shopping, bathing, and housecleaning.
Serving those who have family responsibilities, like those with
elderly parents or young children.
Serving those who lack food, clothes, or a warm place to sleep
*(specify what form this serving might take locally – food bank,
shelter help)*.

Serving those who are undergoing a long course of medical
treatment *(specify what form this serving might take locally –
driving, companionship, etc.)*.
Serving those who are unexpectedly sick.
Serving the bereaved through an offering of practical help and
a listening ear.
We name silently those for whom we pray *(time of silent reflection)*.
"Whoever wants to be first
must be the servant of all."

Serving is the way to greatness.
We give thanks for those in this faith community who offer
specific gifts and skills to help others and to enhance our
worship of God: worship leaders and singers, dancers and
accountants, pianists and artists, teachers and coffee makers,
youth leaders and leaders of health groups for elders, justice
seekers and writers for Amnesty International, listeners and
comfort bringers *(make your own list!)*.
We give thanks for members and friends of this church who
serve in local areas of need.
We give thanks for those who serve through questioning the
way we worship and who we are called to help.
We give thanks for members and friends who serve overseas
faith communities through giving to our mission fund.
"Whoever wants to be first
must be the servant of all."

Serving is the way to greatness. How does our service rate?
What comes first for us, serving our own needs or the needs of
others?
Have we made an inventory of the skills and talents that could
fit us for serving others?
Are we on the lookout for people and causes to serve?
Are we ready to motivate and give confidence to others who
might serve?
Have we the determination to serve over the long haul?
Do we have in mind saints who offer models of service to us,
such as Martin Luther, Martin Luther King, Jr., Mother
Teresa, Jean Vanier, Francis of Assisi?
"Whoever wants to be first
must be the servant of all."

Another Way

1. Sing verse one and the refrain of *When I Needed a Neighbour*
   (*Voices United* #600) before each section, or use all five verses.
   Alternatively, use *The Servant Song* (*Voices United* #595) in
   the same way.

2. Try this abbreviated version. Give advance notice to the
   congregants that you will be asking for their help during the
   prayer.

Serving
the very young without enough support, and the very old
   who are neglected.
Serving
those who lack food, clothes, and housing.
Ask the congregation to shout out the names of local groups.
Serving
friends and family who are chronically ill.
Serving
those unexpectedly sick.
Serving
persons who have suffered loss, persons who are bereaved
   (time of silent reflection).
Loving God, you call us to serve
as Jesus served.

Serving
in the faith community, with gifts and talents.
Ask the congregation to shout out the skills and talents that come
   to mind: for example, worship leaders and singers, dancers and
   accountants, pianists and artists.
Serving
in local areas of need.
Ask the congregation to shout out the organizations and groups
   that come to mind.
Serving
by questioning the ways we worship and who we help.

Serving
by giving to our mission fund. *(Have someone primed to speak
of mission projects.)*
*Loving God you call us to serve
as Jesus served.*

Follow the same pattern for the other sections.

Sunday between September 25 and October 1 inclusive
Proper 21 [26]

LECTIONARY READINGS

Esther 7:1–6, 9–10, 9:20–22 **or** Numbers 11:4–6, 10–16, 24–29
Psalm 124   Psalm 19:7–14

James 5:13–20
Mark 9:38–50

Have the salt of friendship among you and live in peace with one another.

The salt of friendship
Brings those who are in conflict together. We give God thanks for *(current situation)*.
Is seen where teacher and parent work together for the good of a child.
Enables those with differing ways of perceiving the environment to understand each other. We give God thanks for *(current situation)*.
Is certain that a person seeking employment can be helped.
Motivates people to join together to help the very young and the infirm of our community. We give God thanks for *(local care or social initiative)*.
Will work for justice among those with physical or mental challenges. We give God thanks for *(area of action in local or national communities)*.
Zesty friendship
is the beginning of peace.

The salt of friendship
Will question and listen but will not judge.
Encourages the downhearted to tell their story.
Brings a sense of hope to those miserable and depressed.
Knows that laughter in comradeship is potent medicine.
Refuses to believe that a relationship cannot be restored.
Hears the darkest story, yet will not judge or condemn.

Will not leave the sick and troubled in their moments of panic
and despair.
Stays with those who have lost loved ones as they feel their
anger and emptiness *(time of silent reflection).*
Zesty friendship
is the beginning of peace.

The salt of friendship
Welcomes the newcomer but does not smother them.
Gives a faith community member a helping hand.
Accepts the youngest and will not stifle them.
Accepts the elders and listens to their wisdom.
Thanks those who have inspired and given a telling example
in church.
Will not gloss over conflict but faces it head on.
Rejoices in the celebrations and successes of fellow faith
community members.
Includes in their friendship circle members of the wider
church and those helped by mission funds.
Zesty friendship
is the beginning of peace.

The salt of friendship
Enables us to share from the bottom of our hearts.
Frees us to express our thanks.
Restores our faith in ourselves.
Challenges us to stay with another who is going through
a crisis.
Confronts us with the need to change direction.
Is not changed by stress or infirmity.
Remembers the past but is not controlled by the past.
Brings a smile to our face and joy to our hearts.
Zesty friendship
is the beginning of peace.

Another Way

1. Sing the first verse of *Christ, within Us Hidden* (*More Voices*
   #162) or the first verse of *Blest Be the Tie That Binds* (*Voices
   United* #602) before each section.

2. Jesus talks about sins and sinners.

There are sins and there are sinners.
Persons who govern to make themselves rich and powerful.
  We think of *(current persons)*.
We thank God for the brave ones *(current example)* who stand
  up to them.
There are sins and there are sinners.
Persons who could care less about the way we leave our planet
  for our children and grandchildren. We think of *(current
  names)*
We thank God for wise and vocal environmentalists *(current
  example)* who stand up to them.
There are sins and there are sinners.
Persons who believe that money rules supreme. We think of
  (current names).
We thank God for those who are concerned for the well-being
  and dignity of working people, those who are without
  work, and for those who are retired. We think of *(current
  examples)*.
There are sins and there are sinners.
Persons who are indifferent to the particular needs of
  those who walk by wheeling, and those who have mental
  challenges *(local examples)*.
We thank God for those challenged ones who are advocates
  and activists.We thank God for those who advocate on their
  behalf *(names)*.
Our faith in Jesus
runs counter to both sin and sinner.

There are sins and there are sinners.
Faithful ones who do not see or feel the needs of newcomers.
Faithful ones who believe that it is fine to worship only in our
  own place.
Faithful ones whose vision of church ends at the boundaries
  of the local faith community.
Faithful ones whose faith does not encompass justice and
  support for the oppressed.
Faithful ones who cannot bring themselves to reach out a
  hand of friendship to those of other faiths and those without
  a faith.

Our faith in Jesus,
Runs counter to both sin and sinner.

 There are sins and there are sinners.
And we are sinners.
We put off today what we can do tomorrow.
We hang back from saying the words that make a difference,
   like, "Thank you," and "I'm sorry."
We seek for self and neglect community needs.
We enjoy our friendships, but find it difficult to stay the
   course when the testing time comes.
We rejoice in our gifts and talents but are reluctant to try out
   new skills.
We profess our faith in Jesus Christ but shrink from
   Christian action.
We are sinners, but you, Loving God, will have mercy on
   us. Amen.

Sunday between October 2 and October 8 inclusive
Proper 22 [27]

LECTIONARY READINGS

Job 1:1, 2:1–10   **or**   Genesis 2:18–24
Psalm 26   Psalm 8

Hebrews 1:1–4, 2:5–12
Mark 10:2–16

Jesus blesses the children.

Children are a blessing to our world.
Hungry children call us to speak out and act so that hunger
   is banished from our planet.
**Bless us with the will to share from our plenty,
   Loving God.**
Child soldiers call us to root out violence wherever we find it.
**Bless us with the desire to resolve our conflicts
   peacefully, Loving God.**
Children living on the streets and abused in the family home
   call us to advocate for the resources to safeguard them.
Bless us with an anger that insists action is taken.
Children living in slums and tenements call us to speak out for
   decent housing.
**Bless us with the will to press for low-cost housing in
   our town/city.**
You have blessed us with children, Loving God.
Encourage us to stay the course for them.

Children are a blessing to our locality and family.
Where there is lively daycare for children and watchful after-
   school care for students,
your blessing is found, Loving God.
Where there is thorough prenatal care and skillful midwives
   and doctors,
your blessing is found, Loving God.
Where there is the joy of adoption and the gentle foster care of
   young ones,

your blessing is found, Loving God.
Where the concern of those who cannot have children is
recognized, and their giving in other ways supported,
your blessing is found, Loving God.
Where hospitals employ trained pediatricians and specialist
children's nurses,
your blessing is found, Loving God.
We pray for children who are special to us: our own children,
our grandchildren, nieces, and nephews *(time of silent
reflection)*.
We pray for children who are sick at home and in hospital,
and for others in our families and church family who are
suffering *(time of silent reflection)*.
You have blessed us with children, Loving God.
Encourage us to stay the course for them.

Children are a blessing to the church.
Their laughter keeps us from taking ourselves too seriously.
They are God's blessing.
Their simple questions about God and Jesus test our beliefs
and our ability to state them clearly.
They are God's blessing.
Their natural concern for one another and for the
environment is wonderful.
They are God's blessing.
Their understanding of the needs of children far from this
place challenges our giving for mission.
You have blessed us with children, Loving God.
Encourage us to stay the course for them.

Children are a blessing to each one of us.
In the joy and celebration of birthdays and visits in our family
circle,
your blessing is found, Loving God.
Where the needs of children and grandchildren are met, and
their point of view taken to heart,
your blessing is found, Loving God.
Where we are able to talk with and help our children, and
where we are able to hear the needs of other people's
children,
your blessing is found, Loving God.

Where we can identify and heed the needs of the child within
each one of us,
your blessing is found, Loving God.
You have blessed us with children, Loving God.
Encourage us to stay the course with them.

Another Way

1. Sing *Jesus, Friend of Little Children* (*Voices United* #340)
between sections.

2. Today is Worldwide Communion Sunday. Focus on the table of
celebration, and children.

We gather round the table of celebration.
**Bread is broken, the cup is shared, and we remember
Jesus.**
**Jesus worked to bring justice and peace, and our world
is still a place of conflict and injustice.**
Youngsters are still conscripted into armies.
Boys and girls still live on the streets.
Mothers are still at risk.
Children with autism and attention deficit disorder do not get
the help they need.
Hunger is still a reality; breakfast programs are still essential.
Children still live in unhealthy places.
In the bread eaten and in the cup poured out,
we know the will of Jesus Christ for change.

We gather round the table of celebration.
**Bread is broken, the cup is shared, and we remember
Jesus.**
**Jesus worked to bring healing in his time, and suffering
is still a present reality.**
Some children are denied the opportunity to express their
deepest fears and uncertainties.
Some children do not get the daycare and learning
opportunities they need.

Some children do not have the loving bond with parents that
frees and supports them.

Some suffering children are denied adequate medical services.

Some parents have to sacrifice the care of children in order to
put food on the table.

We pray for children who are sick at home and in hospital,
and for others in our family and church family who are
suffering *(time of silent reflection)*.

We pray for parents whose child has died, and for all who are
bereaved *(time of silent reflection)*.

In the bread eaten and in the cup poured out,
we know the will of Jesus Christ for change.

We gather round the table of celebration.
Bread is broken, the cup is shared, and we remember
Jesus.

Jesus worked within a loving community of disciples,
and we still seek compassionate faith communities.

Communities where children's hopes, dreams, and questions
are taken seriously.

Communities alert to the conditions of the world in which
children and grandchildren grow up.

Communities where the younger generation's music and
means of communication *(like texting and Facebook)* are
noticed and used.

Communities where opportunities for sport and discussion
are present.

In the bread eaten and in the cup poured out,
we know the will of Jesus Christ for change.

We gather round the table of celebration.
Bread is broken, the cup is shared, and we remember
Jesus.

Jesus worked to make sure that each individual, rich
or poor, old or young, sick or well, was noticed and
helped.

Each one of us needs to be valued.

To feel that our opinions matter and will be taken to heart.

To believe that our contributions are valuable contributions,
at home, at work, and within our circle of friends.

To be unafraid to forgive or be forgiven.

To be sure that what we offer to our children in terms of play
and sport and creative ideas has love at the centre of it.
To venture into fresh areas of endeavour if it will bring joy to
ourselves and others.
In bread eaten and in the cup poured out,
we know the will of Jesus Christ for change.

---

3. Sing the second verse of *Long Ago and Far Away* (*More Voices* #195) or the refrain of *Eat This Bread and Never Hunger* (*Voices United* #471) after each section.

Sunday between October 9 and October 15 inclusive
Proper 23 [28]   Thanksgiving Sunday

LECTIONARY READINGS

Job 23:1–9, 16–17   **or**   Amos 5:6–7, 10–15
Psalm 22:1–15   Psalm 90:12–17

Hebrews 4:12–16
Mark 10:17–31

The rich man who came to Jesus looking for affirmation.

Reflect on recent positive events in your community and the wider world, and include them in your prayer. Events could include the opening of a new hospital, the start of a service for at-risk children, the rebuilding of a town after an earthquake, or the release of a kidnapped aid worker.

You have given us riches beyond imagining. We give thanks and we celebrate.
The harvests from fields, factories, offices, and institutions have been gathered in.
Peace and stability have been maintained in our nation.
Our loved ones from far away have gathered and we have met in laughter and news-sharing around the table.
As we give thanks, we also remember the failed harvests, the unrest and rioting in other countries, and the families where loved ones cannot be reunited *(time of silent reflection)*.
**Creator God, giver of every good gift,
we thank you.**

You have given us riches beyond imagining. We give thanks and we celebrate.
Many have received skilled and careful treatment in hospitals and clinics.
Many have begun exercise, weight control, and fitness programs.
Many have taken the first step to counter addiction to drugs, alcohol, or overeating.

Many have emerged from the void of bereavement.
As we give thanks, we remember persons who have had
   frustrating delays to treatment, those who have failed to
   maintain a fitness regime, persons who have dropped out
   of AA, and those whose grief goes on and on *(time of silent
   reflection)*.
Creator God, giver of every good gift,
we thank you.

You have given us riches beyond imagining. We give
thanks and we celebrate.
We rejoice in worship and praise in this sanctuary Sunday
   by Sunday.
We rejoice that we have had book studies and Bible studies,
   and begin to know each other so much better.
We rejoice in the children who smile and laugh their way into
   our hearts.
We rejoice that we support the wider church through meetings
   and mission funds.
As we give thanks, we remember persons who through
   infirmity have not been able to attend worship, who cannot
   see the point of learning together, and children denied the
   chance to be a part of any faith community *(time of silent
   reflection)*.
Creator God, giver of every good gift,
we thank you.

You have given each one of us riches beyond imagining.
** We give thanks and we celebrate.**
We celebrate the joy we find in the presence of family and
   good and straight-talking friends.
We celebrate the freedom to worship, read newspapers, vote,
   e-mail, and search the Internet.
We celebrate the ability to work, be a part of social groups, and
   participate in sports and leisure activities.
We celebrate the awesome gift of life itself, in this time and in
   this place.
As we give thanks, we remember troubled members of our
   family and friendship circle, sthe restrictions that curb our
   freedom, and the experiences in work or leisure groups
   that have proved frustrating and challenging *(time of silent
   reflection)*.

Creator God, giver of every good gift,
we thank you.

Another Way

1. Sing the first verse of *Now Thank We All Our God* (*Voices United* #236) or verse one of *We Give Our Thanks to God* (*More Voices* #187) before each section.

2. An eyes-open prayer. As you go through the prayer, add items to be thankful for onto the Communion table. If they overflow onto the floor, so much the better! The object is to show how much we have to thank God for.

You have given us riches beyond imagining.
We give thanks and we celebrate.
We thank you for the opening of a new business and the employment it provides *(manufactured goods or brochures are placed on the table).*
We thank you for our new hospital *(a bedpan and gown are placed on the table).*
We thank you for the harvest from field and garden *(add flowers in a vase and assorted vegetables and fruit).*
We thank you for work and leisure activities *(add coveralls, a laptop, baseball bat, etc.)*
We thank you for loved ones gathered for Thanksgiving *(a family comes to the front and stands around the table).*
As we give thanks, we remember the failed harvests, the unrest and rioting in other countries, and the families where loved ones cannot be reunited *(time of silent reflection).*
Creator God, giver of every good gift,
we thank you.

You have given us riches beyond imagining.
We give thanks and we celebrate.
We rejoice in worship and praise in this sanctuary Sunday by Sunday *(place a hymn/song book and Bible on the table).*
We rejoice that we have had book studies and Bible studies,

and begin to know each other so much better *(hold up and place study books on the table)*.

We rejoice in the children who smile and laugh their way into our hearts *(have a church youngsters' group come into the sanctuary singing or playing together)*.

We rejoice that we support the wider church through meetings and mission funds *(have local faith community representatives come to the front, one holding up a sign with her position printed on it, another bearing money)*.

As we give thanks, we remember persons who through infirmity have not been able to attend worship, those who cannot see the point of learning together, and children denied the chance to be a part of a faith community *(time of silent reflection)*.

Creator God, giver of every good gift,
we thank you.

---

3. **Congregational Experiences**
The worship leader asks the congregation to shout out what they want to thank God for. If what they are thankful for can be put into concrete form, the person may come to the front and place an item on the table (for example, the photo of a grandchild). Another person jots down what is said and offers the prayer, including the bid and response below at the end of each section.

Creator God, giver of every good gift,
we thank you.

Note:

Rather than being quiet and orderly, this prayer experience should be informal, busy, noisy, and fun!

Sunday between October 16 and October 22 inclusive
Proper 24 [29]

LECTIONARY READINGS

Job 38:1–7, (34–41)   **or**   Isaiah 53:4–12
Psalm 104:1–9, 24, 35   Psalm 91:9–16

Hebrews 5:1–10
Mark 10:35–45

The requests of James and John to have the top places beside Jesus.

Do you want to be seen as better than others?
Some captains of industry want to be seen as more capable than other industry leaders.
Many dictators of developing nations want to have more power than anyone else.
Some leaders of political parties want to be seen as more attractive than other party leaders.
Some sports stars want to be seen as the unrivalled player in their field.
Some actors refuse to admit that others could perform with more feeling or vigour.
Friends lacking self-confidence want to come across as superior.
We think of *(examples in the news).*
Jesus has words for them:
If one of you wants to be great, you must be the servant of the rest.

Do you want to be seen as better than others?
Some social or sports group leaders feel they are superior to their rivals.
Some family members think that they have a right to tell other family members what to do.
Some medical professionals are reluctant to refer because they have a false sense of their own ability.
Some patients refuse treatment because they believe they know better than their physician.
Some persons who have lost a loved one affirm, "I'll be over my loss in no time!"

We remember those we know who are sick or bereaved *(time of silent reflection).*
Jesus has words for them:
If one of you wants to be great, you must be the servant of the rest.

Do you want to be seen as better than others?
Some churches boast of superior facilities, choirs, or ministers.
Some church leaders know the way it has always been done.
    And that's the right way!
Some ministers will not share worship or visiting with their congregants.
Some church members believe in the priority of giving to the local church over missions in this country and overseas.
Jesus has words for them:
If one of you wants to be great, you must be the servant of the rest.

Do you want to be seen as better than others?
Do you look down on others in your work or social groups?
And do you convey your opinions to others?
Do you ignore cheeky children or repetitive older folk?
Do you lose patience with those who are slower on the uptake than you are?
Do you covet a superior place in the family circle, or in your sports or leisure time group?
Are you ready to "damn with faint praise" a person who is competing with you?
Do you go out of your way to associate with the "top people,'" or "name drop" when talking with your friends?
Jesus has words for you:
If one of you wants to be great, you must be the servant of the rest.

Another Way

1. A prayer drama.

Dr. Dave Jones: Well, my job is more important than yours. People come to me with life-threatening illnesses. It wouldn't be much good if they brought a bleeding person to your church office!

Rev. Jim Smith: True, but when that same person is dying, your prescription won't be worth the paper it's written on. She'll need someone who speaks of life that goes on when earthly life is over. She'll need a priest or minister. Who will be the important one then?

Nancy Pravic: Cut it out you two! Stop trying to out-do one another! You both have God-given gifts. You use them at different, equally important times. The key question is whether you are willing to serve needy persons carefully and compassionately when the occasion arises.

Jake: You got it wrong again! Like how many times do I have to tell you how to do this machine maintenance job? Just follow the procedures the way I told you and you can't get it wrong. Josie, I don't think you are ever going to reach my abilities when it comes to servicing this machine.

Josie: Jake, the problem with you is that your way of servicing is five years out of date!
The whole servicing procedure was reviewed at the training school and I want to make it clear that the way I do it is far superior.

Fred: What is the most important thing here? The most important thing is that the machine functions well and runs smoothly. Without it the whole production line grinds to a halt. You two are serving the whole operation. So Jake, maybe there is something you will be able to learn from Josie's time at the training school. And Josie, maybe the old dog can teach you a few new tricks.

Follow the same pattern for the other sections.

2. Sing verse five of *The Church of Christ in Every Age* (*Voices United* #601) or the refrain of *Jesu, Jesu, Fill Us with Your Love* (*Voices United* #593) after each section.

3. Focus on the gifts we have received, rather than comparing ourselves to others.

With the gifts you have given to us, O God, come responsibilies.

With the gifts of learning and knowledge come insight and the need to speak up for needy groups in our local community.

With the gift of age comes the wisdom of maturity and the need to be open to fresh experiences.

With the gift of loving partnership comes security and the call to watch out for those who are alone.

With the gift of money comes the sense of security in the family and the opportunity to share with the needy.

O God, Great Giver,
help us to shoulder our responsibilities joyfully and carefully.

With the gifts you have given us, O God, come responsibilities.

With the gift of justice comes the ability to see injustice and work for change.

With the gift of health comes the need to steward our diet and maintain our fitness.

With the gift of concern comes the need to pray for and practically support those who are sick and afraid.

With the gift of friendship comes the call to comfort those who have lost loved ones and bring hope to the bereaved *(time of silent reflection).*

O God, Great Giver,
help us to shoulder our responsibilities joyfully and carefully.

With the gifts you have given to us, O God, come responsibilities.

With the gift of faith community comes the call to reflect on your Word for us in our time and locality.

With the gift of our brothers and sisters in faith comes the need to encourage and care compassionately.

With the gift of leadership comes the need to support and give thanks.

With the gift of the national and worldwide church comes the call to recognize need and give generously.

O God, Great Giver,
help us to shoulder our responsibilities joyfully and carefully.

 With the gifts you have given us, O God, come responsibilities.

Give us wondering eyes to reflect on the profusion of your gifts in creation.

Give us the willingness to protect your gifts in creation and keep them good.

Give us the fulfillment that comes through discovering your gifts in ourselves, and the willingness to use them.

Give us the joy of sharing our gifts with our family, our friends, and with fellow members of this faith community.

O God, Great Giver,
help us to shoulder our responsibilities joyfully and carefully.

Sunday between October 23 and October 29 inclusive
Proper 25 [30]

LECTIONARY READINGS

| Job 42:1–6, 10–17 | **or** | Jeremiah 31:7–9 |
| Psalm 34:1–8, (19–22) | | Psalm 126 |

Hebrews 7:23–28
Mark 10:46–52

Jesus heals the blind beggar Bartimaeus.

Open our eyes, Creator God.
We see the rolling hills, mountaintops, open prairie, the beauty
of lake and ocean, and we give thanks.
We see the scars of opencast mines and industrial waste, and
we long for change.
Open our eyes, Creator God.
We see people fulfilled in their work, happy with the measured
pace of retirement, and active in their sports and social
groups, and we give thanks.
We see workers at risk of injury in their place of employment,
retirees wishing they had the focus and comradeship of
work, and persons frustrated by a leader of a social group,
and we long for change.
Open our eyes, Creator God.
We see refugees being resettled, and those with different
physical and mental abilities finding useful jobs, and we
give thanks.
We see women fleeing armed conflict, their children being
abused, and those with physical and mental challenges
unable to get work and enter restaurants and washrooms,
and we long for change.
We see,
we reflect.
   Do we have the courage to act?

Open our eyes, Compassionate God.
We see diabetics controlling their condition, and others once
obese living at a healthy weight, and we give thanks.

We see those who will not follow the doctor's instructions, or
keep to an exercise or diet program, and we long for change.
Open our eyes, Compassionate God.
We see older persons who have found fulfillment in retirement
activities, those who are strong supporters of family and
friends, and we give thanks.
We see residents in care homes parked in front of the
television, and caregivers being worn out by those with
dementia, and we long for change.
Open our eyes, Compassionate God.
We see those who are dying find God's peace, and those who
have lost loved ones come to terms with grief, and we give
thanks.
We see those who are afraid of dying and those for whom
it seems that grief will never end, and we long for change
(time of silent reflection).
We see,
  we reflect.
    Do we have the courage to act?

Open our eyes, Faithful God.
We see churches where prayer and praise is uplifting and
joyful, where study groups question the Bible and theology,
and we give thanks.
We see churches where the service changes little and learning
is not promoted, and we long for change.
Open our eyes, Faithful God.
We see churches where the newcomer is gently welcomed,
where the troubled faith community member is sensitively
supported, and we give thanks.
We see churches where people keep with those they know and
acts of pastoral caring are only for those in hospital, and we
long for change.
Open our eyes, Faithful God.
We see faith communities that support the needs of local
community groups with gifts of time and enthusiasm, and
we give thanks.
We see local churches who believe that building and local
fellowship needs are what matter most, and that outreach to
the community and mission projects have second place, and
we long for change.

We see,
  we reflect.
    Do we have the courage to act?

Open the eyes of each one of us, Loving God.
We have friendships that have stood the test of time and given
  us joy and strength in the tough times, and we are thankful.
We have old habits and out-of-date ways of seeing the world
  gripping us, and we long for change.
Open the eyes of each one of us, Loving God.
We have found comfort in the faith of our fathers and
  mothers, we have known faith community members there
  for us when the tough times came, and we are thankful.
We have relied too much on the traditional ways of worship
  and prayer, and avoided fresh ways of going on spiritual
  pilgrimage, and we long for change.
Open the eyes of each one of us, Loving God.
We see your presence with us revealed in scripture and in the
  faithfulness of countless saints down the ages, and we are
  thankful.
But we shrink back from saying the words of truth and acting
  out the deeds that would mark us as one of your faithful
  ones, as a follower of Christ.
We see,
  we reflect.
    Do we have the courage to act?

Another Way

1. **Sing verse three of *O for a Thousand Tongues to Sing* (*Voices United* #326) or sing verse one of *Open My Eyes, That I May See* (*Voices United* #371) before each section.**

2. **An abbreviated prayer.**

Jesus opens our eyes.
We see God's glory reflected in forest and field and lake.
And we also see the landscape scars and the pollution of
  Mother Earth.
Jesus opens our eyes.

We see the joy of fulfilling work, travel in retirement, and
friendly social groups.
And we also see hazardous workplaces, poorly led social
groups, and bored retirees.
Jesus opens our eyes.
We see the resettlement of refugees, and useful work for those
of different abilities.   ·
And we also have refugee families without food or hope, and
challenged persons excluded from job opportunities.
We see,
  we reflect.
    Do we have the courage to act?

 Jesus opens our eyes.
We see diabetics who have controlled their condition, and
obese persons now working out and being careful with
their diet.
And we also see persons who do not follow their doctor's
instructions, and those who think an exercise program is a
waste of time.
Jesus opens our eyes.
We see older persons who are happy and fulfilled in their
own homes, and elders who pass on wisdom to their family
members.
And we also see older persons parked in front of the
television, and the caregivers of those with dementia being
worn out.
Jesus opens our eyes.
We see those who are dying find God's peace, and those who
have lost loved ones come to terms with grief.
And we also see fear in the eyes of the dying, and those for
whom it seems grief will never end.
We see,
  we reflect.
    Do we have the courage to act?

Follow the same pattern for the other sections.

Sunday between October 30 and November 5 inclusive

Proper 26 [31]

LECTIONARY READINGS

Ruth 1:1–18   **or**   Deuteronomy 6:1–9
Psalm 146   Psalm 119:1–8

Hebrews 9:11–14
Mark 12:28–34

*Love the Lord your God with all your heart...
and your neighbour as you love yourself.*

Love God, and love your neighbour.
Is my neighbour the country where many lack a regular
   supply of food or clean water?
Is my neighbour the child who sleeps on the streets in Delhi,
   Jakarta, or San Paulo?
Is my neighbour the physically challenged person who is
   denied access to a church or restaurant because there is no
   elevator or ramp?
Is my neighbour the person who looks for support in the
   search for employment?
Is my neighbour the young mother juggling family
   responsibilities and a full time job?
Who is my neighbour? It is a hard question.
Jesus says, "Love your neighbour as you love yourself."

Love God, and love your neighbour.
Is my neighbour the person who is depressed and despairing
   and needs me to listen?
Is my neighbour the child who wants to share a game or needs
   help with her reading?
Is my neighbour the person next door who is sick yet lacks the
   courage to see her family doctor?
Is my neighbour the friend in hospital who needs to share her
   frustration and fear?
Is my neighbour the close companion who has lost her beloved
   spouse and needs to share her feelings of anger and loss?
(time of silent reflection)

Who is my neighbour? It is a hard question.
Jesus says, "Love your neighbour as you love yourself."

Love God, and love your neighbour.
Is my neighbour the person who comes through the church
  door for the first time?
Is my neighbour the local community person who has a vague
  longing for a "spiritual life" but has no church connection?
Is my neighbour the fellow church member who is going
  through a time of personal struggle?
Is my neighbour someone in the church locality who would
  like to start a community kitchen? *(or other community
  project)*
Is my neighbour someone supported by mission funds whose
  name and challenges I neither know nor experience?
Who is my neighbour? It is a hard question.
Jesus says, "Love your neighbour as you love yourself."

Love God, and love your neighbour.
Is my neighbour the family member looking for emotional or
  practical support in hard times?
Is my neighbour the friend for whom life is no longer fulfilling
  and fun?
Is my neighbour the person speaking up for a cause to which
  we could give time and energy in the coming months?
Is my neighbour the disappointed member of the local
  immigrant community?
Is my neighbour one whose needs are screamed from the
  headlines or whispered over the garden fence?
Who is my neighbour? It is a hard question.
Jesus says, "Love your neighbour as you love yourself."

Another Way

1. Sing a verse of *When I Needed a Neighbour* (*Voices United*
   #600) before each section of the prayer.

2. Sing verse three of *Christ, within Us Hidden* (*More Voices*
   #162) after each section.

3. Sing the chorus of *Jesu, Jesu, Fill Us with Your Love* (*Voices United* #593) before and after the prayer. Dialogue with the congregation around the question, "Who is my neighbour?" Use the four sections to form the prayer, and have a second worship leader write down and offer the prayer. Sing a verse from the hymn between sections.

4. Make the prayer affirmative.

We love God and we love our church neighbours.
Newcomers are ours to love.
Spiritual seekers are ours to love.
Fellow members in trouble are ours to love.
Neighbourhood groups seeking a home are ours to love.
Faith communities served by our mission funds are ours
     to love.
*Who is **our** neighbour? It is a hard question.*
Jesus says, "Love your neighbour as you love yourself."

Family members in trouble are ours to love.
Friends for whom life is a burden are ours to love.
Deserving causes that could use our help are ours to love.
Newcomers to our country are ours to love.
Those with crying need are ours to love.
*Who is **our** neighbour? It is a hard question.*
Jesus says, "Love your neighbour as you love yourself."

Follow the same pattern for the other sections.

Sunday between November 6 and November 12 inclusive

Proper 27 [32]

LECTIONARY READINGS

| Ruth 3:1–5, 4:13–17 | **or** | 1 Kings 17:8–16 |
| Psalm 127 | | Psalm 146 |

Hebrews 9:24–28
Mark 12:38–44

The sacrificial offering of the poor widow.

When celebrated as Remembrance Day, Armistice Day, or Veterans Day, preface the prayer with this section.

Give sacrificially,
and remember those who served in land or sea or air forces:
Some young men and women gave their lives,
some young men and women gave their mental and physical
   health,
some gave up promising careers, or family life,
some grew and matured through the experience,
and some never recovered from it *(time of silent reflection)*.
We remember and we are thankful for their sacrifice.
We will give to help them.
We will give understanding,
give of our time,
give of our special talents,
give of our material resources.
We will give and we will receive.

Give sacrificially
to help the starving and the homeless. We think of *(current
   need)*.
To support the youngest and the most vulnerable. We think of
   (current need).
To stand alongside the downtrodden and forgotten. We think
   of *(current need)*.
To halt and reverse the degradation of our bio-system. We
   think of *(current environmental concern)*.

We will give understanding,
give of our time,
give of our special talents,
give of our material resources.
We will give and we will receive.

Give sacrificially
to care for those who in losing a job have lost self-respect,
to support those for whom life seems hollow and tasteless,
to stand with those for whom pain is an everyday reality,
to hear the heartache of those who in hurting others have hurt
    themselves,
to bring peace to those who have lost a loved one *(time of*
    silent reflection).
We will give understanding,
give of our time,
give of our special talents,
give of our material resources.
We will give and we will receive.

Give sacrificially
to support your friends in faith community,
to show the relevance of your church through what you say
    and what you do,
to give leadership in finding and meeting local needs,
to help, through mission funds, those whose names you will
    never know but who will be forever grateful *(time of silent*
    reflection).
We will give understanding,
give of our time,
give of our special talents,
give of our material resources.
We will give and we will receive.

Give sacrificially.
Our friends may laugh at our "foolishness."
Our critics may say, "They are to be despised!"
Our families may question our priorities.
We may gain nothing in the eyes of the world *(time of silent*
    reflection).
But we will give understanding,

We will give of our time,
We will give of our special talents,
We will give of our material resources.
We will give and we will receive.

Another Way

1. Sing *What Does the Lord Require of You* (*Voices United* #701) or *What Can I Do?* (*More Voices* #191) before each section.

2. Use examples of modern-day sacrifice in the prayer.

 The offering of two coins doesn't seem like very much, but it is a sacrificial gift.
A business executive leaves his million-dollar-a-year post to build homes for low-income families.
A politician goes against party guidelines to vote for a clean air bill, and is thrown out of caucus.
A trusted employee blows the whistle on a situation where health regulations are being ignored and loses his job.
A company buyer turns down a large bribe and gives the contract to the lowest bidder *(time of silent reflection)*.
Sacrificial gifts,
but a priceless, faithful return.

 The offering of two coins doesn't seem like very much, but it is a sacrificial gift.
A daughter turns down an out-of-town promotion to help care for her aging parents.
A mother persists in her efforts to get special education for her mentally challenged son and receives abuse and contempt for her pains.
A lawyer spends time and money defending a prisoner whom he believes has been wrongly convicted, and loses paying clients in the process.
The spouse of a loved one who has died is unable to come to terms with her grief and is suspended from her job.
We pray for those who have sacrificed and suffered.
We pray for those who are sick and those who are bereaved *(time of silent reflection)*.

Sacrificial gifts,
but a priceless, faithful return.

NOTE:

If there is a current situation in the local or national news where sacrifice has been costly for an individual, mention the name and the incident in the prayer.

Follow the same pattern for the other sections.

Sunday between November 13 and November 19 inclusive

Proper 28 [33]

LECTIONARY READINGS
1 Samuel 1:4–20   **or**   Daniel 12:1–3
1 Samuel 2:1–10   Psalm 16

Hebrews 10:11–14, (15–18), 19–25
Mark 13:1–8

Jesus warns that a change beyond imagining is coming.

Creator God, we worry about radical change.
We see the effects of climate change in flooding more
    extensive than any in living memory.
We see the effects of devastated fish stocks and hear the
    experts say, "The fish will never return to the seas and
    oceans."
We see the effects of global pollution: overflowing landfills and
    floating garbage dumps covering miles of ocean.
We see the effects of deep-rooted unemployment boiling over
    into riots and political instability.
We see declining population in some countries and the
    inability to curb population growth in others *(or other*
    situations in the local or national news).
The signs of radical change cause us to fear the future *(time of*
    silent reflection).
But you, our wise God, call us to watch, wait, work, and
    speak for positive change.
In your strength, we face the challenges and forces of
    despair head-on.

Compassionate God, we worry about radical change.
We are uncertain about the increasing speed and the variety of
    ways of communicating with others.
We are familiar with the growing complexity of family life and
    the different configurations of "family."
We know about the shorter time each child has to enjoy play
    and sport before she or he is considered grown-up.

We are aware that there are ingredients in our staple
  foodstuffs that make cancer and heart disease more likely.
The reality of the increasing shortage of diagnostic equipment
  in our hospitals comes home to us.
The growth in the number of persons requiring institutional
  care concerns us.
And we remember now those in our church family and in our
  family and friendship circles who are in pain, bereaved, or
  concerned for their future *(time of silent reflection)*.
*But you, our wise God, call us to watch, wait, work, and
  speak for change.*
**In your strength we face the challenges and forces of
  despair head-on.**

Compassionate God, we worry about radical change.
Families are shopping and youngsters going to hockey and
  baseball games instead of church on Sunday morning.
Funerals have become secular celebrations, and many
  weddings are held outside the sanctuary.
There is now an emphasis on personal meditation and
  spiritual quest, and faith community study is replaced.
Ministry has been devalued as a vocation, and fewer persons
  are studying at theological college.
Fewer persons in church means that less money is given to
  support mission projects *(time of silent reflection)*.
*But you, our wise God, call us to watch, wait, work, and
  speak for change.*
**In your strength we face the challenges and forces of
  despair head-on.**

Compassionate God, we worry about radical change.
The continuing revolution in computers and the social media
  leaves us breathless and uncertain about the future.
The need to train and then retrain for employment is
  confusing to us.
The gathering violence in our communities causes us to fear.
The lack of respect of the young for the old, and the old for
  the young, bewilders us.
The lack of certainty in so many areas of life is perplexing to
  us: change happens too fast *(time of silent reflection)*.

But you, our wise God, call us to fresh understanding,
to patience in the confusion of new ideas, and to the
willingness to embrace new visions.

Another Way

1. Sing *Sent Out in Jesus' Name* (*More Voices* #212) after each section.

2. An abbreviated prayer using the response "radical change" and allowing more time for reflection.

Radical change.
The dramatic effect of climate change. We think of *(give current examples)*.
(Time of reflection.)
Landfills overflowing, oceans where floating garbage dumps are a reality. We think of *(give current examples)*.
(Time of reflection.)
Radical change.
Riots and protests because there are not enough jobs. We think of *(give current examples)*.
(Time of reflection.)
A fast declining population in the Ukraine and Russia *(give current examples)*
but exploding populations in Haiti and Egypt.
(Time of reflection.)
Radical change is the reality.
Give us understanding, O God, and a visionary response.

Radical change.
The growing complexity of family relationships, and the shorter time that boys and girls can laugh and play as children.
(Time of reflection.)
The revelations about harmful food ingredients and the ways livestock are raised.
We think of *(give current examples)*.
(Time of reflection.)

Radical change.

The shortage of affordable essential drugs and the time delays for diagnostic procedures and elective surgery. We think of *(give current examples)*.

The shortage of places for those who require personal care because of increasing infirmity and dementia.

(Time of reflection.)

And we remember now those in our church family and in our family and friendship circles who are in pain, bereaved, or concerned for their future.

(Time of reflection.)

Radical change is the reality.

Give us understanding, O God, and a visionary response.

Follow the same pattern for the other sections.

Reign of Christ or Christ the King Sunday

Proper 29 [34]

LECTIONARY READINGS
2 Samuel 23:1–7   **or**   Daniel 7:9–10, 13–14
Psalm 132:1–12, (13–18)   Psalm 93

Revelation 1:4b–8
John 18:33–37

The King who speaks the truth.

This is the truth:
If the way of Jesus ruled, all children would have enough food,
a safe place to live, and an education.
This is the truth:
If the way of Jesus ruled, the developed nations would share
their plenty equally, women would not be abused, and gays
and lesbians would feel safe.
This is the truth:
If the way of Jesus ruled, immigrants would have appropriate
jobs and those from minority cultural groups would be free
from discrimination.
This is the truth:
If the way of Jesus ruled, prisoners with mental illness and
addictions would receive thorough treatment and then be
eligible for parole.
Come Jesus, come just and compassionate Jesus.
**It's your way for our hearts, your way for our church,
your way for our world.**

This is the truth:
If the way of Jesus ruled, basic health care would be available
to every person in every nation.
This is the truth:
If the way of Jesus ruled, the very old would be respected for
their wisdom, and the elderly infirm would be treated as
well as babies and young children.
This is the truth:
If the way of Jesus ruled, money could not buy superior health

care and the waits for diagnostic procedures and elective surgery would be over.

This is the truth:

If the way of Jesus ruled, those who have lost loved ones would be comforted and given the time they need to grieve *(time of silent reflection)*.

Come Jesus, come just and compassionate Jesus.

It's your way for our hearts, your way for our church, your way for our world.

This is the truth:

If the way of Jesus ruled, the church would care more about fellowship and less about its buildings.

This is the truth:

If the way of Jesus ruled, sign language would be commonly used in worship and resources in Braille would be readily available. All sanctuaries would be wheelchair accessible.

This is the truth:

If the way of Jesus ruled, the relevance of the church would be self-evident and its central mission place would be outside the halls and sanctuary.

This is the truth:

If the way of Jesus ruled, givers of mission money would encourage and seek feedback from the recipients *(time of silent reflection)*.

Come Jesus, come just and compassionate Jesus.

It's your way for our hearts, your way for our church, your way for our world.

This is the truth:

If the way of Jesus ruled, we would care more for the poor and disadvantaged.

This is the truth:

If the way of Jesus ruled, our priorities for spending tax money would have the marks of justice and care-full-ness all over them.

This is the truth:

If the way of Jesus ruled, we would not be afraid to publicly affirm our loyalties.

This is the truth:

If the way of Jesus ruled, love would rule in our family circle, love would permeate our friendships, and love would show in everything we do *(time of silent reflection)*.
Come Jesus, come just and compassionate Jesus.
It's your way for our hearts, your way for our church, your way for our world.

Another Way

1. Sing verse one of *Rejoice, the Lord Is King* (*Voices United* #213) or *The Kingdom of God* (More Voices #146) before each section.

2. Engage the congregation in a dialogue around the way the world, suffering persons, and the church would be different if Jesus ruled. A second worship leader would formulate a prayer from the dialogue.

3. Offer ways to make the reign of Jesus a reality.

Jesus reigns!
Shy people and those who are slow to make their presence felt are noticed.
The work of hospital cooks, cleaners, and porters is appreciated.
Physiotherapists and x-ray technicians, laboratory workers, and those who make prostheses are valued.
The depressed and downhearted find courage.
Those who suffer chronic pain find relief.
The sick who are reluctant to go to the doctor do so, and those who bother medical people for no good reason are told to stay away.
The dying are embraced with peace, and the bereaved gently supported *(time of silent reflection)*.
Will Jesus reign in our time?
We will bring his reign closer!

Jesus reigns!
There is a caring faith fellowship. The building serves church members and friends; church members do not serve the building.

Those who are challenged because of their mental or physical conditions are welcomed and find the resources they need.

Members who are in leadership roles are appreciated and thanked.

The Good News is communicated to the neighbourhood in ways that are in tune with contemporary lifestyles.

Gifts for mission and community projects overseas are greater than those for the local faith community *(time of silent reflection)*.

Will Jesus reign in our time?
We will bring his reign closer!

Follow the same pattern for the other sections.

THEMATIC INDEX

Please note that the page numbers refer to the first page of the Sunday in which that theme is represented.

HEBREW SCRIPTURE INDEX

NEW TESTAMENT SCRIPTURE INDEX